Fantasy Football:
The Next Level

Fantasy Football:
The Next Level

HOW TO BUILD A CHAMPIONSHIP TEAM EVERY SEASON

David Dorey

WARNER
BOOKS

NEW YORK   BOSTON

Warner Books
Hachette Book Group USA
237 Park Avenue
New York, NY 10017

Visit our Web site at www.HachetteBookGroupUSA.com.

Warner Books and the "W" logo are trademarks of Time Warner Inc. or an affiliated company. Used under license by Hachette Book Group USA, which is not affiliated with Time Warner Inc.

Printed in the United States of America

First Edition: August 2007

10 9 8 7 6 5 4 3 2 1

Library of Congress Cataloging-in-Publication Data

Dorey, David.
    Fantasy football : the next level : how to build a championship team every season / David Dorey. — 1st ed.
        p. cm.
    Summary: "The foremost authority in fantasy football presents his first ever comprehensive guide to seeing past the statistics and into heart of the game's strategy."—Provided by the publisher
    ISBN-13: 978-0-446-69925-9
    ISBN-10: 0-446-69925-X
    1. Fantasy football (Game)   2. Fantasy games.   I. Title.
    GV1202.F34D67 2007
    796.332—dc22   2006038993

Dedicated to my son, Brian

Believe in yourself
Challenge yourself
And always face the sun

Acknowledgments

Any book is the product of long hours spent left alone, but it is only through the love and support that my wife, Karin, and son, Brian, have given that allows me a career in a field that most people consider only as a pleasure. It's never a solitary pursuit knowing that the meaning of life is just down the hallway.

I was once described as a jack of all trades and a master of most (no, really, I was). For that I would most need to thank my parents. Somehow I inherited both my father's sense of analytical perfection and my mother's love of writing and humor. Put them together in the Internet age and you get a Web site, even if they still struggle to explain to their friends what I do for a living.

I would also be remiss in not recognizing my friend and business partner Whitney Walters, who nudged me in a local draft in 1996 and mentioned "we should open a Web site." The Huddle has been a huge part of my life for over a decade now and remains my passion and purpose. It would have never been possible without Whitney's vision and hard work, nor would it have been as thoroughly enjoyable and life-changing. If it all went away tomorrow, it would always be the most exciting thing I have done.

This material banged around in my head for a few years but it took teaming up with my literary agent, Byrd Leavell III, to recognize the possibility after we fleshed out the bones that would become this book. The reality was realized thanks to Warner Books for giving me the only thing in life I've ever really wanted—an opportunity.

Lastly I must thank the thousands of Huddlers from the past decade who have graciously given me a reason to stay up late nights pounding away on the keyboard doing what I love to do. I have greatly enjoyed interacting with you all on the message board, on the phone, via e-mails, and even in person. Lou Gehrig was the first to say it and I may not be the last, but I honestly believe I am the luckiest man in the world.

Contents

Prologue: Because Once Is Not Enough

Chances are pretty good that you are holding this book while wondering if it could help you become a better fantasy team owner. You've played fantasy football before so you don't really need to know how to create a league, make up rules and schedules, or conduct a draft. You have already learned all those basics and probably did pretty well in the past. Maybe you won your local league. Perhaps you even did well in a large contest. Regardless of where you are coming from, you're just wanting to take your skills and knowledge—and therefore fun and entertainment—to The Next Level. While almost anyone armed with a cheat sheet can luck into some surprise player and a "magic year," you want more than a hot tip about some sleeper this year. You want to be the best team owner in the room both before and after the season. And again next year. And the next.

Fantasy Football: The Next Level was written for you.

I've played fantasy football for close to two decades now and have been the Senior NFL Analyst for TheHuddle.com for over 10 years. While perhaps my bread and butter there is advising people on who to draft each summer and later which players to start each week, there are far larger dynamics at play in fantasy football. Most people approach a fantasy draft as if it were a chance to pick the winner of 16 consecutive horse races. It isn't. As any savvy fantasy team owner can attest, the best rosters will have not only as many top players as possible but also depth for future needs and players that will either remain good or improve as the season progresses. Their roster is strategically created to build the best total team. A hot start is a major advantage but the best finish wins the league.

If you are still fairly new to fantasy football, this book is filled with tools and insights to better understand your fantasy team. Everything contained in these pages is the product of many years of research, analysis, and experimentation. *The Next Level* will help you build a better team, manage it more wisely, and go deeper into your playoffs than ever before. There are 25 rules discussed through the course of the book intended to summarize the general dynamics that will affect every fantasy team. Only by understanding them can you ensure that the effect is always positive for you.

If you are a fantasy football veteran with a wallful of trophies and the reputation of being "the guy to beat" in your league, this book is especially for you. I've written so much about the basics of fantasy football over the years and spent so much time dwelling on the immediate situation in the NFL every year that this book was a breath of fresh air to write. *The Next Level* was written so that even the most experienced fantasy football fanatic will get something out of every single chapter. Be it a new tool, an insight, a statistical breakdown, or whatever, every chapter delves into the finer aspects of the hobby and offers samples based on actual statistics and NFL results over the past 10 years. It's not enough to just tell you something—you deserve to have it broken down and proven. More than anything, I wrote this for the guy who already knows quite a bit and yet realizes that he can never know enough.

The premise of this book is all about playing at The Next Level. What is true in this book you are now holding was true five years ago and will be true five years from now. The underlying principles and trends in the NFL do not change from year to year, and even in the rare event that they do, you'll find the tools to recognize and understand what is new. Improving your skills and fantasy teams is a never-ending process (and delightfully so, I will add). Oh yeah, I'm sure that you're already good. The only question is: Do you want to be better?

Introduction: The Other Side of the Goal Line

Back on a late-summer day in 1970, I gathered with about 20 other fourth-grade boys to form a Pee Wee football team. I already loved football to be sure, but I didn't yet know how it was really played. I only knew that I wanted to participate in a sport that seemed to be popular, fun, and actually encouraged me to bash into other people. After we took a knee in front of the dads-turned-coaching-gods, we listened as our head coach, Mr. Henderson, stood before us casually spinning a football in his hands.

"So who can tell me what football is all about?" he asked.

Being only nine years old, we didn't know enough to say endorsements, hot chicks, or signing bonuses. After listening to a few futile attempts regarding snow cones or serving the unfulfilled lives of our fathers, Coach Henderson held out the football.

"It's very simple. Football is about one thing—the other side of the goal line. We get this ball on the other side of their goal line, we score. We let them bring it across our goal line, they score. At the end of the game, biggest score wins."

Woo-hoo! We're ready! Let's play! Let's play!

We figured that was about all we needed to know. Football, like any sport not involving Tiger Woods, is just about scoring more points than your opponent. It was true thirty years ago, and it is true today.

Fantasy football is no different. It too is a competition that uses the results from players in professional football games to determine which fantasy team has more points each week. The utter beauty of it is that instead of traveling all over the country and dealing with hostile crowds, we gain our points while at home, sitting at a sports bar, or even while we take the kids to the county fair on Sunday so they can ride something appropriately named "The Vomit Blaster."

Okay, so participating in professional football in this manner may not bring millions of dollars or national fame. But at least we get a chance to own a handmade trophy, and maybe enough cash for a night out with the spouse to make up for all the weekends spent watching games. For leagues made up of co-workers, it also means that every Monday morning only half the guys are thinking, "God, I hate working here" (though they hate it even more than usual).

And so now you, I, and millions of other people are playing fantasy football. And we all know that fantasy football is about scoring more points than our weekly opponent. But how much further have we taken our involvement beyond just knowing that fantasy football is about the other side of the goal line? It's just about picking players that score a lot of points, right? The team with the most player points at the end of the game wins, right?

Sure. At the most basic level, that is always true. But as with any competition that becomes more refined and sophisticated, there's much more to the game than simply understanding the main goal. Fantasy football can be nothing more than using a listing of players and picking a team before the season starts—and for many people that's all they do, and that's okay. But for others, like you, there is more to learn and do to improve a fantasy team's fortunes every year.

This book is offered as a way to blast through the learning curve for people who are still relatively new at fantasy football. It also offers tips, insights, tools, and information that can help even seasoned veterans improve already formidable abilities and knowledge. This book is not about the hot running back for this year or what particular quarterback to avoid. This is not about the new crop of players this year. Reaching The Next Level is not just knowing about individual players in a specific season; it is about arming yourself with the knowledge and insight to understand the unique aspects of your league, your scoring system, and how to best create your team—not merely with a collection of names left at the top of the list you tore out of a magazine or copied off the Internet.

We'll travel through the four areas of the fantasy football cycle—the off-season, the preseason, the regular season, and, in case you have never been there before, that small collection of games at the end called the playoffs. For many fantasy team owners, all that matters is the preseason draft and then using those players during the season. But the more devoted team owner comes to realize one rather important, and yet somewhat overlooked, component to owning a fantasy team—that you own "a team." Not merely a listing of players, but a related group of players who have to address the unique aspects of your specific league in the way they are drafted and how they come together on a weekly basis to provide you with the optimal fantasy score.

Let's run down the fantasy football cycle that we'll be considering:

The Off-season This is the downtime of the year because you have no team, right? It is if you want to remain with the cheat sheet masses that wait until the week before the draft to catch up on the NFL. You do have a team; it just does not have any players yet. You still are part of a league (or will be), and this time of year should be used to understand your league as it relates to your team. That means doing a bit of analysis on those unique starting and scoring rules that set the later stage when you finally fill your roster with players.

Every league has some combination of scoring rules, roster limits, and weekly starting requirements. The variations can be endless, and yet there is only one scenario that is of any importance to you. The only one that matters is how your particular league scores player performances, how many players are on your fantasy team, and which positions you will be starting every week. Until you understand the unique nature of that, you are just worrying about the other side of the goal line without knowing how best to get there.

You cannot draft a team intelligently without knowing the true value of positions to your total team. This becomes critical because while you are picking individual players, everyone else in your league is as well. All too often they are taking the same players you have your sights on. It doesn't really matter if you know a handful of surefire, cannot-miss sleepers who will win your league if you cannot draft them first. Reaching The Next Level is about team first, positions second, and only after that—actual player names.

Not to worry, there are ways to attain that knowledge without impeding on your plans to visit the Bahamas or preparing for your next audition for *American Idol*. The biggest bang for the buck comes well before you start to formulate strategies to grab specific players. It is when you spend just an hour or so understanding your team and league better. Entering your draft without understanding the unique nature of your league is like going to the auto parts store without knowing the make and model of your car.

"Yes sir, I am looking to buy something to make a car go fast. I mean really fast. My car is named Nut Crushers. And I want something that was shiny last year."

The Preseason   Training camps open and preseason games are on television to whip up the fantasy football fever! Never mind that you will not recognize some of the names of the players because, within a month or so, many of them will be back to building patios. There is football on the television. Life is improving all the time.

Preseason is for preparing for your draft and determining how all those players should be ranked and pursued. It's time for making player projections, checking out mock drafts, and creating your own killer cheat sheet. Armed with the knowledge gained from just a few off-season activities, you can intelligently build that team that respects your league and scoring rules. We'll look at the basic truths of NFL players that increase your odds of getting the right players for your team.

This is the most exciting time of the year because no fantasy teams have lost a game and, as far as they think, they are about to draft their best team yet. Only a few will, of course, and those will be the teams that respect the uniqueness of their league and accumulate players who make the optimal set of starters.

The Draft   There's little as much fun as a fantasy draft, and amid the camaraderie, trash talking, and false bravado you'll be picking players for your team. Every round you get to select any NFL player—but only if he hasn't already been picked. The biggest challenge is not about knowing which players will do well for the year; it's about making an optimal pick when you finally get the chance to draw from the ever-dwindling supply of unclaimed players. Tools like mock drafts, tiering, and the Advanced Draft Tracker will allow you to plan ahead and be able to quickly react as your draft uniquely unfolds.

You'll be making critical decisions in those early rounds that will have a great impact on what you can, if not must, do in later rounds. A fantasy draft is not about picking players as if they were horses in a race, because all positions are not equal and your aim is to create an optimal set of starters. Before you sit down in your draft, you must know what your intentions are on grabbing positional starters, with enough flexibility planned that you can react to fortuitous events like players you covet dropping to you that you had not expected. Aside from all the work on ranking players, a draft is a mini-world all its own that will never be the same between any two leagues. The draft wouldn't unfold the same way if it were just delayed a day.

The Regular Season   This is the time to continually monitor your roster for upgrades. The process begins with the first kickoff of the season and ends only when the waiver wire is closed for the year. The NFL is a dynamic collection of 32 teams that are always changing as players rise and fall in production, others get injured, and the schedule gets tougher or easier.

No NFL team ends with the same depth chart that they had to start the year—neither should your team. Churning your roster can be the road to staying a step ahead of disaster and, even better, a way to constantly improve your set of starters every week. Sweetest of all—you can grab players you don't even need but other league mates could have used against you.

"Gosh—you wanted him too? And to think I don't really need him!"

Every season has fantasy teams that appear to be a league monster (based on last year), only to float down the standings as expectations are not met and a few critical injuries or changes to NFL teams spell disaster outside the realm of their control or reasonable anticipation. Doesn't matter—you have to assume you will own that team every year and never stand pat. You'll get points from starters scoring—it doesn't matter who the players are or when or how you obtained them. And you never get points for what he did the previous season.

The Playoffs Nothing matters if you do not get to the playoffs, and yet, you must continue winning through the final game. Learn how to anticipate a playoff run without affecting your chances to get there. Just like in the regular season, it doesn't matter if you have different players in every position at the end; all that matters is getting starter points.

Once you understand the fantasy football cycle and embrace the unique nature of your individual league, you'll find that you can build and manage a far better fantasy team and possibly even take less time to do it because you will better understand what is important and what is not.

That first year that you played, did you go to your draft with no more preparation than a list of names to pick? If all the time you spend is on player names, have you really gone beyond that first year? Are you really any better at fantasy football?

Fantasy football is about players, to be sure, but it is about so much more than that. It is about a team—your team. It is about players—but only your players. It is about gaining an edge beyond the individual names called out on a fun-filled night in August. If you're happy just picking names and letting it ride, more power to you and I hope to see you in my leagues. If you want to gain advantages, understand what it means to own a fantasy team in all aspects, and have more fun with fantasy football than ever before—perhaps you are ready.

Welcome to The Next Level.

THE Off—season

UNDERSTANDING YOUR LEAGUE USING LAG

Question: What feat did Emmitt Smith accomplish three times but Terrell Davis only managed once in his career?

Answer: Both runners led the NFL in rushing yards in the same year that they were on the winning Super Bowl team. Larry Brown managed to reach the Super Bowl in 1972 with the Redskins but they lost, as did Shaun Alexander with Seattle in 2005. This means that 36 times over a 40-year period, having the most productive running back did not translate into winning the league championship.

HOW CAN THIS BE? We all know that running backs are the big guns for offenses and that having a good rushing game in the NFL, like in fantasy football, is paramount to winning championships. How can it be that having the most productive tailback in the entire league was not enough to reach and win the Super Bowl 36 times in the first 40 years? And not even once in the first 26 years of the league championship?

The truth for the NFL is no different from the truth of your fantasy team—one player does not make for an entire team. Even if you had a magical crystal ball that could guarantee which player would be the highest scorer in your fantasy league that year, would that alone be enough to win? Probably not. And oh yes, that assumes you even had the chance to draft him. Your weekly success comes directly from the total fantasy points from ALL of your starting players combined going against the lineup of your opponent. The point to fantasy football is not to have the highest-scoring player (though, hey—don't we all love that), it is to have the highest-scoring team each week.

The first step to reaching The Next Level is to understand how your fantasy team scores points. All fantasy leagues do not use the same scoring rules and many like to change every season. It all matters. A team that may win a championship handily in one league may struggle to reach the playoffs in another depending on how fantasy points are awarded. You cannot build an optimal team until you understand two very critical aspects of your league scoring—how it affects player values within a position and how it affects positions compared to each other.

After a decade of working at The Huddle Web site and having been in contact with literally thousands of fantasy owners, the most common advantage that I have seen in fantasy leagues pertains to understanding the league scoring. It is an area that those who make the rules occasionally use to their own great benefit by drafting differently from the more casual owners. While certainly not all leagues have rule makers with nefarious intentions, playing fantasy football at The Next Level means approaching every draft differently unless, by some odd chance, those separate leagues have the exact same league rules.

The reality is that the majority of fantasy players only rely on the previous season's statistics from their league to determine their rankings and draft plans. That is an obvious and important tool to use for understanding your league, but most think of it by names and numbers. Figure 1.1 is an example of what someone could have seen at the end of the season in their league.

What most fantasy owners in that league would immediately believe is that they need to grab two running backs, since they have the highest scores, then a quarterback, and then eventually a couple of wide receivers before settling on a tight end. Grab the kicker and defense when the runs start on those positions. They then arm themselves with a player ranking that looks suspiciously similar to

SAMPLE LEAGUE SCORING—TOP 10 PER POSITION

Quarterbacks	Running Backs	Wide Receivers
252 C Palmer	358 S Alexander	228 S Smith
243 T Brady	328 L Johnson	200 L Fitzgerald
228 E Manning	307 L Tomlinson	194 S Moss
228 P Manning	299 T Barber	193 C Johnson
223 M Vick	260 E James	182 T Holt
222 D Bledsoe	237 C Portis	181 A Boldin
216 D Brees	220 R Johnson	181 J Galloway
214 B Favre	220 I Jordan	179 C Chambers
214 M Hasselbeck	195 M Anderson	177 M Harrison
213 K Collins	195 T Jones	159 H Ward

Tight Ends	Kickers	Defenses
164 A Gates	165 N Rackers	171 Bears
125 J Shockey	162 J Feely	156 Panthers
119 T Heap	138 S Graham	154 Colts
113 A Crumpler	134 J Wilkins	151 Giants
112 C Cooley	133 J Kasay	145 Steelers
105 J Witten	133 L Tynes	138 Broncos
95 T Gonzalez	128 M Vanderjagt	136 Seahawks
83 R McMichael	126 J Elam	133 Vikings
79 L Smith	126 R Lindell	130 Ravens
78 J Stevens	124 J Brown	129 Jaguars

Figure 1.1

the statistical results of last year and go into their drafts with the express aim to build a killer team based on the previous season. This brings up the first important rule of fantasy football:

Rule 1

Draft your team for this year, not from last year.

While this idea will be much expanded on later, this is likely the biggest weakness and most natural tendency of fantasy team owners, young and old. As your expertise increases, it becomes enlightening to watch other team owners draft as if they are armed with nothing more than the stats from last year. They are picking those highest-scoring players from the previous season while knowing that they could have a monster team—if only they had a time machine that could go back 12 months.

Setting up your draft for THIS year is done by first forgetting about individual players and initially focusing on the team that you will build. To do this you must understand the effect that fantasy scoring rules have on positions, and the best way to accomplish that is with a League Analysis and Graphing (LAG). A quick and relatively easy process, a LAG can open your eyes about the unique characteristics of your league and should be a mandatory activity even if you do nothing more than pick up a cheat sheet on the way to your draft.

What you will need is a listing of the top 20 scorers in all positions used in your league from the previous season. If this is a new league for you, then you'll need to have that scoring scenario applied to the previous year's statistics. There are numerous ways to access this information:

1. Use the data you should already have from the previous year if applicable.

2. For joining existing leagues, ask a member from last year for the information.

3. For new leagues, use an online or desktop league management product that can generate the numbers for you. Many allow free use in the preseason.

4. Figure them all out manually, or use the power of a spreadsheet to calculate them using a formula against last year's stats.

A spreadsheet can be a very powerful tool and well worth the investment in time and effort to learn at least the basics of its use. Plus if you have a desk job, you can use a spreadsheet for fantasy football analysis while at work since it certainly looks better than surfing the Web or playing online poker when your boss walks past. There are numerous places on the Internet to access at least the raw stats, including The Huddle, and you can easily just copy them from the Internet and paste them into a spreadsheet.

Considering a very basic scoring system that rewards touchdowns and yardage but no reception points, and basic scoring for kickers and defenses, it could end up looking similar to this sample season:

SAMPLE LEAGUE RESULTS FOR TOP 20 SCORERS—QB, RB, WR, TE, PK, AND DEF

Rank	QB	RB	WR	TE	PK	DEF
1	252	358	228	164	165	171
2	243	328	200	125	162	156
3	228	307	194	119	138	154
4	228	299	193	113	134	151
5	223	260	182	112	133	145
6	222	237	181	105	133	138
7	216	220	181	95	128	136
8	214	220	179	83	126	133
9	214	195	177	79	126	130
10	213	195	159	78	124	129
11	211	189	156	76	124	127
12	208	181	153	69	123	126
13	205	167	145	66	120	126
14	192	166	145	64	120	121
15	183	164	142	61	116	119
16	183	163	141	60	116	119
17	172	162	139	55	111	118
18	163	161	139	52	108	116
19	162	155	132	44	108	116
20	156	152	131	44	106	116

Figure 1.2

Using the previous year's stats allows the best accuracy, but the reality is that in any given year almost the same thing happens in position scoring. The top three scores in each position may vary but the differences between the others are minimal. Every year, the differences between the fifth, 10th, 15th, and 20th highest scorers rarely exceed 2 percent or 3 percent. The names change but the numbers rarely do. In the event they do change—usually because of a new league scoring condition or a significant rule change in the NFL—performing this type of analysis will keep you as up to date as possible.

While these numbers alone could be used for a review of position and player value, the power of a spreadsheet lets us move one easy step further to give us an immediate view of how this particular scoring scenario has affected the player values. After highlighting the above table (figure 1.2) and clicking on the graphing button, a line graph can be easily drawn that would yield the table in figure 1.3.

Now that we have a graphical expression of the top 20 players in each position, we can proceed to do a League Analysis and Graphing. There are two critical aspects of a graph to understand—how quickly player values diminish within each position and how positions compare to each other. Once you learn how to create a LAG for your league, it is a quick and easy process that should be done each year for every league you are in. Quite simply, it shows everything you need to know about player value in your particular scoring system for all positions that you will be drafting and later starting each week.

Many fantasy players become so engrossed in generating their own player projections and rankings that they overlook how past season stats apply to fantasy positions in their unique league scoring rules. A player at The Next Level understands what positional value is all about before worrying about which name to call in August. It may fly in the face of the player-centric NFL these days,

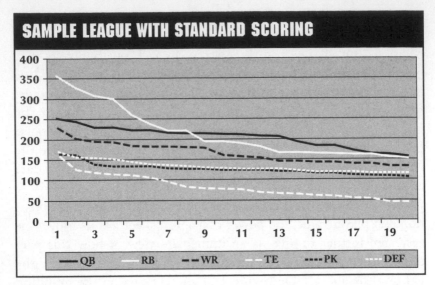

SAMPLE LEAGUE WITH STANDARD SCORING

Legend: QB — RB — WR — TE — PK — DEF

Figure 1.3

but reaching The Next Level means understanding *in order* the three components that matter most—team first (rules and requirements), position second (comparative values), and player names third. A bit backward from how most view fantasy football but important enough to become our second rule:

Rule 2

Success is about team first, positions second, and players third.

Getting the stud fantasy player is an obvious benefit to your team, but unless your league only starts one player each week, that's not enough to win. In the NFL, only five times in the first 40 years has the most productive running back in the league been able to hold the Lombardi Trophy in January. It's all about the team and winning the championship, not just having the best player. What exactly is *your* goal every season?

LAG ANALYSIS: FANTASY SCORING BY POSITION

"Raw statistics are like a girl in a bikini. Sure, it is revealing but it often takes a lot more work before you can see everything."

MOST FANTASY TEAM OWNERS are familiar with statistics, and those numbers are easy enough to review and determine which position is the highest-scoring. Then again, most fantasy owners also end up around .500 on their season and out of the playoffs. There are more to those numbers than many realize.

The NFL produces roughly the same number of fantasy points per position every season. Using a basic fantasy scoring system that awards .05 point per passing yard and three points per passing touchdown, consider a five-year block of quarterback scores (see the next page).

The biggest variation we see here is with the top three players. That will hold true for literally every other position. Each season produces at least two or three top players that are significantly better than the rest, and their fantasy points will rise and fall far more than the other spots along the lines for season production. Basically, the top three will either turn in big years or they will turn in monster years.

Certainly you could use an averaged set of numbers, but the return is not significantly different from just using the previous season. This brings up our next rule, which is critical to remember when dealing with statistics:

Rule 3

Statistics—whether actual or projected—
are only useful as guidelines.

Remember, we are interested in what is behind the statistics. Consider the top 20 scores for quarterbacks from a sample season:

1	298
2	281
3	263
4	253
5	250
6	244
7	241
8	239
9	233
10	228
11	221
12	218
13	212
14	204
15	196
16	193
17	183
18	182
19	176
20	168

And the resulting graph (see figure 2.1).

In reviewing each position, there are two characteristics of interest.

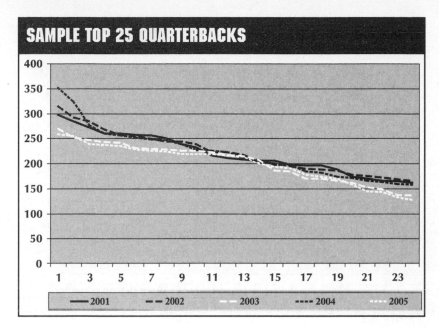

SAMPLE TOP 25 QUARTERBACKS

2001 — 2002 — 2003 — 2004 — 2005

Figure 2.1

1. How steeply the line declines over the set of players.

2. Any portions of the line that create a natural tier, or significant drop-off to the next player.

The angle of descent of the line indicates how quickly value is lost from having the first, 10th, or 20th best quarterback. Using the sample above, it's easy to see that having the best quarterback is worth about 50 points more than the fourth best in this scoring scenario. If we waited and hope to rely on the 15th best quarterback, you know you are giving up about 100 points in this scoring scenario. But the line is steep only for those first three players or so; otherwise the decline is gradual. Good things to know when we later compare positions and determine which positions we need to draft in what order.

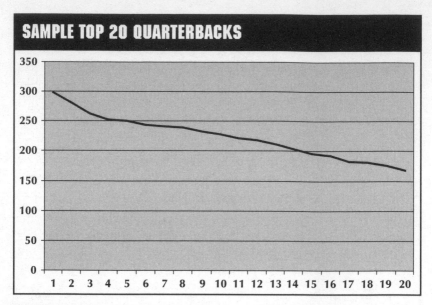

Figure 2.2

For this example, there is a natural tier after the fourth best quarterback—there aren't any other significant drop-offs. In other positions and using different scoring rules, quite often there are other natural tiers and occasionally they can be dramatic. In this particular sample, the angle of descent is largely smooth and consistent, which suggests that selecting your quarterback in a draft can be done strategically because you will already know what the point effect of waiting longer will be, particularly when you know what teams already have quarterbacks and how many are likely to be taken between your current pick and next pick.

After viewing the graph, there is one other step to perform that makes the reality of this scoring situation more clear—it will be especially useful later when we are comparing positions.

3-10-20 ANALYSIS

Using the top 20 scores for the position, a breakdown can show even more. By averaging the top three scores, the fourth through 10th and the 11th through 20th highest scores show what the difference truly is in your league for your particular scoring rules (see figure 2.3).

A 3-10-20 analysis is one of the best tools for determining how value declines in a position in your fantasy scoring scenario. Why average? Because there is almost always a top three tier for a position and the 4–10 numbers are representative of the rest of the starters drafted in your league. The 11–20 numbers are the backup/second tier players that team will have on their rosters. This may seem to beg the question "why not make it 3-12-24 for a 12-team league?" You can—the difference is not that significant. The primary purpose of these tiers is simply to understand the differences between great, good, and backup-quality quarterbacks without being blinded by your personal preferences on individual players.

The sample shows that burning that early pick on a quarterback will net you around 280 points for the season. Waiting a bit longer is a decrease, but only about 40 points or so in this particular scoring scenario. Delaying your starter until the first dozen or so are taken will likely cost you around another 50 points per season. In this sample, the difference between a top quarterback (280 points) and waiting until the starter run is over (195) is going to mean giving up roughly 90 points in a season or around five or six points per week (at least). This is assuming you get an average (those ranked 4–10) quarterback. As we will discuss later, the consistency and reliability diminish far faster than total numbers will.

In different scoring situations, the graphed line can be sharply declining, which means the better the player you get in that position, the more advantage you will have. In other scoring rules the line could almost become flat, which screams out that taking an early player in that position makes virtually no sense at all if there

SAMPLE TOP 20 QUARTERBACKS USING TOTAL FANTASY POINTS

1	298	Average = 280
2	281	
3	263	
4	253	Average = 241 or about –40 points
5	250	
6	244	
7	241	
8	239	
9	233	
10	228	
11	221	Average = 195 or about –85 from top 3
12	218	
13	212	
14	204	
15	196	
16	193	
17	183	
18	182	
19	176	
20	168	

Figure 2.3

are other positions to draft that will net you a far higher overall gain.

The same goes for natural tiers. It is not at all uncommon for tiers to be created for the top three, then again around the eighth to 10th spots, and again around the 20th spot. What is important is that you know what your specific league scoring rules do to player statistics.

Performing a LAG graph and then a 3-10-20 analysis provides you with the invaluable knowledge of how valuable players are within a position. It can give you a realistic feel for how value declines within a position and what you gain or give up when you make your selection of a top, average, or below-average player. The numbers don't change much from season to season, just the names do. Understand the position first, and you will better recognize what value a player is bringing to your team.

Fantasy players love statistics. The problem is they can be easy to get lost in and can even become misleading taken by themselves. Performing a LAG literally shows you how your specific scoring system relates to NFL players. The process can be done in a few minutes once you are familiar with reproducing the numbers into a graph and pulling out the three levels of players for review.

The LAG is crucial for recognizing natural tiers produced by your scoring system and adjusting your strategy to that reality, but, as important as it is to understand value within a position, it pales in comparison to the value of knowing how positions compare to each other. The LAG and the 3-10-20 analysis are about to get a whole lot more revealing.

LAG ANALYSIS: SCORING BETWEEN POSITIONS

"Heroes trumpet the story of battle but it takes an army to win a war."

WHILE PERFORMING A LAG and a 3-10-20 analysis will yield invaluable information about how player value declines within a position, this alone won't win your league unless it only uses one position. Not likely. Just as the military needs separate branches to wage war, your fantasy team will use various positions each week to produce a point total. It is this total team score that matters, and it is crucial to understand the separate positions both individually AND combined to recognize where player value truly lies for your roster. The goal of a LAG analysis is to know *when* to draft different positions.

Consider the sample league fantasy points (see figure 3.1).

Looks like just a bunch of numbers, really. You can look across each row to see what each relative scorer does in the different positions and it's easy enough to see which positions have the highest scores by glancing at the #1 scorer in each position. But does this always hold true? At what point do positions change their importance relative to all other positions? This sort of number table is not all that useful and can be confusing. Even worse, it can be misleading if we just glance at the #1 scorer in each position and then assume that all positions decline at the same rate.

Turning it into a graph makes the relative values of positions come to life (see figure 3.2).

SAMPLE LEAGUE TOP 20 SCORERS FOR ALL STARTING POSITIONS

	QB	RB	WR	TE	PK	DEF
1	293	341	242	161	151	136
2	276	321	214	137	142	126
3	253	307	197	115	130	118
4	246	292	193	97	124	114
5	244	264	188	94	122	111
6	237	250	185	91	120	105
7	234	243	182	85	119	103
8	233	216	180	79	116	101
9	227	207	174	74	115	99
10	223	203	164	72	113	95
11	222	196	161	69	109	94
12	219	189	159	66	109	92
13	212	180	154	64	107	92
14	204	179	152	60	106	90
15	192	177	150	58	104	88
16	191	175	145	56	103	86
17	177	168	142	52	102	85
18	175	164	141	50	100	84
19	169	161	138	47	99	83
20	163	156	134	45	98	81

Figure 3.1

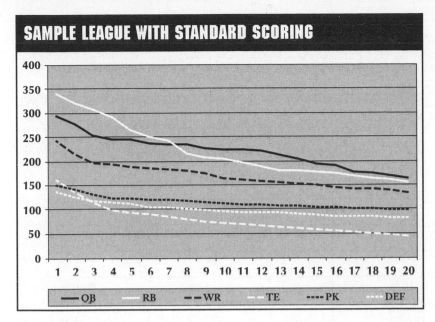

SAMPLE LEAGUE WITH STANDARD SCORING

Legend: —— QB   —— RB   – – WR   —— TE   ···· PK   ---- DEF

Figure 3.2

Now that we have an easy-to-read, graphical expression of what our sample league is about, we can proceed to make comparisons and determine how these specific league scoring rules affect the relationships of the positions used. This graph shows that in this particular league, running backs are prized possessions for the first half dozen or so, and that wide receivers never gain as many comparative points as do the running backs. The first dozen or so running backs are still scoring more than the third best wideout. Other than the top three kickers and defenses, there appears to be minimal difference in owning the fourth best or the 14th best in those positions. And if you are relying on owning a tight end that makes any difference, you better be first or second in line.

Remember—this is true only for this particular league scoring and not necessarily for yours. And our concern for now is just to understand the positions—we'll figure out how to fill in those ranked names within positions later. Breaking the fantasy points per position down into a 3-10-20 analysis, we gain even more insight:

COMPARING THE DECLINE IN SCORING FOR EACH POSITION

	Top 3 Average	4th to 10th Average	Drop 3rd to 10th	11th to 20th Average	Drop 11th to 20th	Drop 3rd to 20th
QB	274	235	39	192	43	82
RB	323	239	84	175	65	148
WR	218	181	37	148	33	70
TE	138	85	53	57	28	81
PK	141	118	22	104	15	37
DEF	127	104	23	87	17	39

Figure 3.3

While we are making our draft plans, it is now evident that the biggest decline in fantasy points comes with running backs (yeah, I know, you already thought that). It is obvious that grabbing a top running back in this scoring system means having an immediate scoring advantage over the rest of the league. It also probably means that you have one of the first three draft picks. As we will discuss in later chapters covering each position, the knowledge gleaned from a 3-10-20 analysis of scoring has to be matched up with the reality of how positions are raided in your league draft.

As far as top players go, this scoring scenario does not suggest that taking an early quarterback will pay much dividend, despite being the second-highest-scoring position. There is only a 39-point advantage to having a top three quarterback compared to having an average starter in this league. So realistically, quarterbacks likely will not be drafted nearly as fast as most other positions here. However, figure 3.3 shows a big advantage from snatching up that top tight end because there is a 53-point drop in waiting outside the top three. This is even more dramatic considering that, outside of those precious few high-scoring tight ends, the graph shows the position is almost worthless.

In this scoring, wideouts consistently are the least declining position outside of kickers and defenses. The difference between a top three wideout and waiting until the first wave is drafted would only cost you a mere 37 points—about two points per week. Wide receivers are a group of players with specific considerations, to be sure, but overall this scoring suggests seeding your roster with them only after securing a couple of running backs and a top tight end if possible.

The kicker scoring used here was just standard points three points per field goal and one point for a successful extra point. Taking into account an overall view of the scoring, they just don't matter much here, nor do defenses in the minimal scoring awarded. Both lines are almost flat, which is borne out in the 3-10-20 analysis by the almost insignificant drops in scoring by waiting on the position. Having the best kicker or defense here versus having one of the worst starters in the league likely only accounts for around two points per game—Oh boy!

This initial review of the league can be revealing about how positions compare and how quickly value declines. Best of all—it applies specifically to your league rules. This is vital, since each fantasy league has unique scoring rules that will affect a LAG, and those positions will roughly score the same each season. You will already know what is going to happen.

To illustrate my point, let's spit out another LAG using different scoring rules. Our previous sample league used fantasy scoring that awarded three points per passing touchdown, six points per all other touchdowns, 0.05 point per passing yard, and 0.1 point per rushing or receiving yardage. Kicker points are standard, and

SAMPLE LEAGUE SCORING USING 1 POINT PER RECEPTION

	QB	RB	WR	TE	PK	DEF
1	309	368	332	253	165	150
2	297	356	301	194	162	148
3	285	352	287	190	138	146
4	273	349	284	183	134	137
5	265	297	281	178	133	134
6	265	285	278	173	133	133
7	262	263	263	171	128	128
8	261	236	263	143	126	128
9	256	226	259	140	126	124
10	253	218	232	124	124	123
11	251	216	230	123	124	123
12	248	207	227	123	123	121
13	242	203	226	115	120	119
14	237	198	218	115	120	118
15	221	196	215	111	116	117
16	208	189	212	103	116	116
17	204	183	209	95	111	115
18	193	181	205	90	108	115
19	190	176	205	85	108	114
20	189	172	202	79	107	113

Figure 3.4

defenses just get sacks, turnover, and touchdown points. The next sample league awards four points for passing scores, one point per 20 yards passed, a negative one point per interception, one point per 10 yards rushed or received, throws in a one- or two-point bonus for longer field goals, and gives points for defenses that hold down opponent points to five or fewer points. And oh yes, the biggest change of all—one point per reception. A sample year produces the scoring in figure 3.4.

Just a couple of scoring changes made some significant differences. Top scores are higher and the differences between positions are already showing major discrepancies. Graphing it out gives a picture much different from our first sample league.

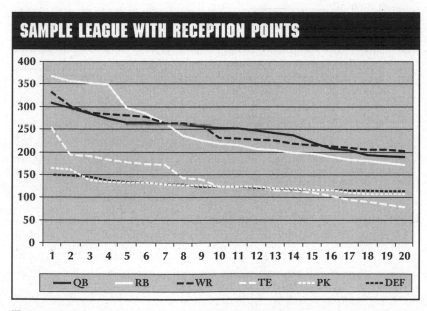

Figure 3.5

There is a lot more natural tiering happening here and some critical differences that this scoring produces compared to the first sample league. There is a major tier happening around the fourth best running back and a sharper decline in the line. Quarterbacks drop off around the fifth best, so getting "early quality" looks like a worthy advantage.

Most important of all—look what just happened to those wideouts! Through the first 16 or so, they are either commensurate or even higher than the running backs. This is quite a change from the first sample league, and one that must figure into draft plans. A natural tier occurs around the 10th best wideout, and amazingly they are already as valuable as running backs in regard to scoring for the critical top 10's in each position. Again—wideouts have some unique characteristics to be discussed later, but I already know that in this league I would not be waiting nearly so long to acquire a high-scoring receiver. While some reality will need to be applied regarding how players are drafted, owning one or more top wideouts in this league will pay much bigger dividends to my total score than in the first sample league.

Those reception points also make tight ends suddenly worth owning, and the top player there is someone to truly covet—he scores about as well as a top 10 running back or wideout. A natural tier also appears around the seventh best tight end, which means grabbing an earlier tight end will also be an advantage in this league. In the first sample league, not owning a top three tight end means no harm in waiting.

Taking this into a 3-10-20 analysis draws another picture different from our initial sample league (see figure 3.6).

Okay, so no major shock here—running backs still decline quickly. But now that early tight end, particularly the top tight end, is the next best value to consider comparing what is lost from dropping from a top three to a top 10 player. While there still remains a need to grab running backs, the wideouts are much more important in this scoring scenario. Considering the decline in the line for running backs compared to wideouts, after owning at least one if

COMPARING THE DECLINE IN SCORING WITH RECEPTION POINTS

	Top 3 Average	4th to 10th Average	Drop 3rd to 10th	11th to 20th Average	Drop 10th to 20th	Drop 3rd to 20th
QB	297	262	35	218	44	79
RB	359	268	91	192	76	167
WR	307	266	41	215	51	92
TE	212	159	53	104	55	108
PK	148	130	18	117	12	31
DEF	155	129	26	115	14	40

Figure 3.6

not two decent running backs those wideouts make more sense to acquire (depending on league tendencies and circumstances).

Our scoring changes to defenses and kickers resulted in higher scores but not a significant change to how they drop in value within the positions. That reception point has done what seemed impossible—made wideouts, and even tight ends, worth grabbing early.

This analysis produces valuable knowledge to apply during drafts. Considering the above sample league, let's say you are drafting third. You grabbed that obligatory running back with your first selection, and 18 picks later there have been 14 running backs, two quarterbacks, and two wideouts already taken. You know that the next running back should be worth around 200 points, the next quarterback about 295 points, the next wideout is about 300 points, and that glorious best tight end worth 250 points is still on the board. Take a second running back there or opt for a quarterback or wideout? Or maybe draft that tight end? Would anyone actually shoot beer out of their nose if you drafted a tight end in the second round? It all depends on factors soon to be considered, but by performing a LAG and a 3-10-20 analysis you already know what the relative values of positions are during those critical initial rounds of your draft.

Because a LAG and 3-10-20 analysis show the true value of positions in your league, they are even more important when your league uses "creative" scoring rules or starts anything other than the standard QB-RB-RB-WR-WR-WR-DEF-PK. Have a flex position to fill? You need to know what the bang for your buck will be six or eight rounds into a draft when you decide what position is best for that optional starting slot. Use individual defensive players? While they perform vastly different tasks on the football field from the offensive players, they all produce the same thing for you—fantasy points. You have to know value to determine the optimal mix of players on your team.

There's plenty more to learn and use to play fantasy football at The Next Level, but you first have to understand how your team needs to come together. And then the fun really begins.

RECEPTION POINTS

4

King Arthur: Go and tell your master that we have been charged by God with a sacred quest. If he will give us food and shelter for the night, he can join us in our quest for the Holy Grail.

French Soldier: Well, I'll ask him, but I don't think he will be very keen. Uh, he's already got one, you see.

King Arthur: What?

Sir Galahad: He said they've already got one!

(From Monty Python and the Holy Grail, *1975)*

IF THE NFL DRAFTED like we do in fantasy football, every college player who did not pass, carry, or catch the ball might as well just go play golf that Saturday because they would have no chance to be drafted. Of course the NFL mixes in all positions when they draft, and while some are merely addressing needs, most are taking the best player they can with those valuable early picks. While fantasy football has the same concept, all too often that translates into a feeding frenzy on running backs in the first if not second round as well. The worst I have seen in my 17 years of playing? The first non–running back went with the 25th pick—the first pick in the THIRD round. Obviously the Holy Grail of fantasy football is the stud running back followed by an average back, which is followed by "I need another running back now!"

That is not only a huge deviation from the way the real NFL drafts happen, it also opens the door to major advantages and disadvantages related to draft position. Drafting last in the first round should be a great spot with a swing pick that nets you the 12th and 13th best players in the draft. As it often works out, that team often just ends up with the 12th and 13th best running backs. Fantasy teams are usually just responding to three big realities: Running backs usually score the most, they will be stripped from the shelves first, and you will need two or three good ones. The most common scoring scenario over the last two decades has been awarding one point per each 10 yards rushing or receiving, six points for touchdowns, and two points for any two-point conversion. Quarterbacks have most often been given the same scoring, with the addition of one point per 20 yards passed and three points per passing touchdown (or four points with a negative point per interception, which works out almost exactly the same for most).

That scoring scenario yields this LAG graph:

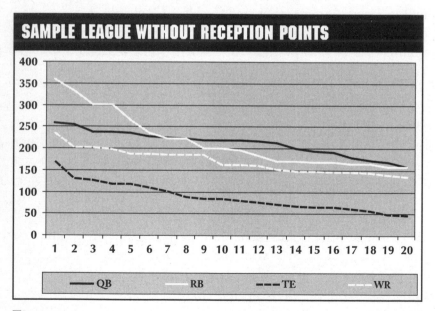

Figure 4.1

The graph bears out why the behavior of fantasy teams is to load up on running backs. They are more valuable than quarterbacks for the first seven players in this scoring scenario and they are always more valuable than a comparably ranked wideout. Throw in the fact that there are far more starting wideouts than running backs in the NFL and the only reasonable thing is to make your draft become a running back orgy for the first two rounds before finally caring that you have perhaps seven or eight other starters every week.

That means those teams in the back end of the first round have to make a pretty tough call. They can either grab a couple of running backs who likely will be little more than average and then hope a few decent wideouts, quarterbacks, or tight ends are still available when they pick again at the next swing pick at the end of the third round. Or they can decide to snap up a top quarterback or wideout knowing that their second running back will likely be a hole they can never completely fill without a bit of good fortune. By the end of the third round in such drafts, there are often 24 or more running backs gone, plus the elite players from the other positions as well. And yes, it is not considered a problem by those drafting at the start of the first round, since it all plays directly into giving them a big advantage.

While anything is fair if everyone agrees to it, the reality in that situation is that you have to be a better drafter than those snobs holding the premier running backs just to make up the difference. It certainly can be done. And those snobs can easily screw up a good thing. But the intent in competing in fantasy football is to have a level playing field. In my nearly two decades of playing fantasy football, I have witnessed advances like separating tight ends from wideouts, adding a flex position, and defensive point awards for points or yards allowed. But hands down, the greatest invention in the history of fantasy football is *reception points*.

Rule 4

Reception points mean fair drafts, better teams, and more competition.

There is no other single scoring change that can accomplish so much to make a draft more diverse and grant reasonably predictable value gains for players based on how many receptions they have. Admittedly, as a purist, I was not initially a fan of them since it seemed a contrived way to score fantasy points that was not as directly related to how well an NFL player contributes to his team as touchdowns and yards. After reviewing the effect and witnessing it in drafts, I am now completely sold on reception points as the greatest invention since the TV remote control.

Reception points began to show up in fantasy leagues around 2000 and were boosted in use by several large contests that had a vested interest in minimizing the advantages of teams with early draft picks. If your league already uses it, I shouldn't have to sell you on it, but if you have not yet played with reception point awards, your league could be more fun and more competitive. Consider the change to the LAG graph (see figure 4.2) when the exact same sample league previously mentioned added one point per reception.

Sure, the first five running backs are still kings—that is almost inescapable short of devising some fairly screwy scoring scenario. But suddenly the top wideouts become comparatively more valuable than running backs starting around the sixth-ranked player. And the disparity becomes larger the further down the lines you go. The first half dozen tight ends are now scoring more than the 20th best running back. Quarterback scoring has not changed but their relative value certainly has.

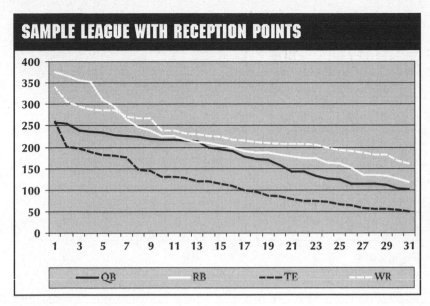

SAMPLE LEAGUE WITH RECEPTION POINTS

Legend: ——— QB   —— RB   ---- TE   ---- WR

Figure 4.2

Breaking it down for a more easily read comparison, the league without reception points would have the highest-scoring 30 players, include only four receivers, and yet have 15 quarterbacks. Already that presents a problem since most leagues are only 10 or 12 teams and those starting quarterbacks will end up equal in scoring to about the first eight or 10 running backs and only one wideout. And no tight ends.

But with reception points, there are only six quarterbacks ranked in the top 30 players and suddenly there are more wideouts than running backs in that grouping. There is even a tight end! Compared to a non–reception points league, there are more options for building an optimal team and a greater incentive to take an early wideout or even a tight end, which prolongs the supply of running backs for everyone.

Considering the first 60 highest-scoring players in a non–reception point league (or an equivalent to the first five rounds of

TOP 30 SCORERS FROM 2 LEAGUE DRAFTS USING DIFFERENT SCORING RULES

Without Reception Points				*With Reception Points*				
Rank	QB	RB	WR	TE	Rank	QB	RB	WR	TE
1–10	4	5	1	0	1–10	0	6	4	0
11–20	7	3	0	0	11–20	2	2	5	1
21–30	4	3	3	0	21–30	4	2	4	0
Total	15	11	4	0	Total	6	10	13	1

Figure 4.3

a 12-team league), the scoring results in 20 quarterbacks, 22 running backs, 17 wideouts, and finally just one tight end. Five rounds into a draft with this scoring and the running backs will have been stripped well in advance of those 22 and yet the wideouts likely won't nearly be at the 17 mark that scoring suggests are most valuable. One person will likely take the plunge on that elite tight end but probably no others will be taken.

Adding in reception points has a wonderful effect. Now there are only 16 quarterbacks ranked in the top 60 highest-scoring players. There are only 16 running backs that have scored that much and yet 25 wideouts are that valuable to own. And even three tight ends have shown up in this scoring. What this should result in at the end of the fifth round in a 12-team league is that there will be a few quarterbacks taken, probably two or three tight ends, and as many wideouts gone as there are running backs (or at least a far closer number). Why would you want to pass up a top 10 wideout that scores as well as a top 10 running back and instead select yet another running back that may not equal the 30th best wideout?

TOP 60 SCORERS FROM 2 LEAGUE DRAFTS USING DIFFERENT SCORING RULES

Without Reception Points					With Reception Points				
Rank	QB	RB	WR	TE	Rank	QB	RB	WR	TE
1–10	4	5	1	0	1–10	0	6	4	0
11–20	7	3	0	0	11–20	2	2	5	1
21–30	4	3	3	0	21–30	4	2	4	0
31–40	3	2	5	0	31–40	5	2	3	0
41–50	1	5	3	1	41–50	2	2	6	0
51–60	1	4	5	0	51–60	3	2	3	2
Total	20	22	17	1	Total	16	16	25	3

Figure 4.4

Reviewing the first 100 highest scoring players without reception points yields 29 quarterbacks (virtually all NFL starters), 31 running backs, 34 wideouts, and finally six tight ends. Since this would be round 10 in a 10-team league or round nine in a 12-team league, you know that everyone has their quarterbacks and may be starting to get their backups. They already have drained out at least 40 or more running backs and finally about the same number of wideouts. They may have taken five or six tight ends. By the ninth or 10th round, this sample league has finally caught up all the teams to about the same rosters, only with some owning a distinct advantage at running back. Those teams with the elite wideouts and tight ends are not as strong as those with better running backs.

But in the sample league with reception points, there are 22 instead of 29 quarterbacks among the top 100 players. That is about

TOP 100 SCORERS FROM 2 LEAGUE DRAFTS

Without Reception Points					*With Reception Points*				
Rank	QB	RB	WR	TE	Rank	QB	RB	WR	TE
1–10	4	5	1	0	1–10	0	6	4	0
11–20	7	3	0	0	11–20	2	2	5	1
21–30	4	3	3	0	21–30	4	2	4	0
31–40	3	2	5	0	31–40	5	2	3	0
41–50	1	5	3	1	41–50	2	2	6	0
51–60	1	4	5	0	51–60	3	2	3	2
61–70	3	2	4	1	61–70	0	4	4	2
71–80	2	2	5	1	71–80	3	3	2	2
81–90	1	2	5	2	81–90	1	2	7	0
91–100	3	3	3	1	91–100	2	2	4	2
Total	29	31	34	6	Total	22	27	42	9

Figure 4.5

equal to the number of starters needed in the league. Running backs fall only marginally from 31 to 27 in the top 100 but wideouts and tight ends are significantly more valuable.

The beauty in this is that those first three to five rounds of your draft suddenly have many more options for building a high-scoring team. By the eighth or 10th round, there is no difference to how your draft will go, but in those critical early rounds, there is no longer the immediate disadvantage of drafting late in the rounds.

There are fewer reasons to make the first two rounds become a "Name the Running Back" game. And for the more astute fantasy player—many more ways to reach that league championship.

Another benefit from reception points is realized every week of the regular season. In the league without reception points, it is almost certain that those teams with the top three running backs are doing well. It is hard to overcome consistently high production from those players as long as their owners have managed to field at least an average team around their stars. But with reception points, now having a stellar set of wideouts can be more advantageous than having a great 1-2 punch at running back. More options to build your team and more ways to end up with the highest score for the week and isn't that what it is all about?

THE EFFECT OF RECEPTION POINTS WITHIN POSITIONS

The addition of reception points has significant benefits to how positions compare to each other, and that only begs the question—does it change how players are ranked within their position? Does it suddenly make wide receiver A rocket up the rankings while wide receiver B only elicits giggles when he is drafted?

Here is the reality. Despite the tendency to refine player values to a tightly defined single set of projected stats, there just is not that much difference within a position ranking when reception points are added. Actually, I've done the math on numerous scoring scenarios and can tell you definitively that the changes in the way players are ranked are minimal at best and can be almost completely ignored at worst. There are a few differences with reception points worth noting, but the tendency of fantasy team owners to significantly shift their rankings when reception points are introduced is largely unwarranted.

RUNNING BACKS

Using standard scoring described previously applied to a sample 2005 season, notice just how little the introduction of reception points actually changes how players were ranked based on scoring for the year (see figure 4.6). Any year will show almost the exact same phenomenon. In this case, the top 20 scoring running backs when there were no reception points were considered.

Realize that not only were there just three players that had a shift of more than two spots, but that this comes from the actual results from that season. It is rather doubtful that your rankings are going to be an exact mirror of the actual results. This suggests that almost no player is worth moving more than two spots in your projections. Over half of them moved no more than one ranked position. Using pure projections to create rankings will certainly result in more movement than this, which is just another reason why player risk, upside, reliability, and consistency must be applied to rankings beyond best-case-scenario statistics.

There is more variation the deeper you go in the running back rankings from 2005, though nothing that surprising. The biggest changes came from players like McGahee and Parker who rarely had any receptions in games. And of course Brian Westbrook, who is one of the rare backs with consistently high receiving catches and yards. But even LaMont Jordan only moved up one spot despite being #1 in running back receptions in 2005. Reception points downgrade goal line backs like Brandon Jacobs or the classic example, Jerome Bettis. But there has to be a very extreme case of either adding a lot of catches or having almost none before it truly affects where a running back falls.

The nicety of reception points with running backs is that it pumps more value into those third-down backs. That won't translate into a starter for you any more than they would have without them, but at least they can offer more fantasy points as a filler for a bye week or a worst-case replacement. Reception points do make

CHANGE IN ACTUAL RESULTS WITHOUT AND WITH RECEPTION POINTS—RB'S

Rank	Without Rec Pts	Running Back	New Rank	With Rec Pts	Change in Rank
1	360	S Alexander	1	375	0
2	333	L Johnson	2	366	0
3	302	T Barber	3	356	0
4	301	L Tomlinson	4	352	0
5	266	E James	5	310	0
6	235	C Portis	7	265	-1
7	224	L Jordan	6	294	1
8	223	R Johnson	8	246	0
9	200	T Jones	10	226	-1
10	199	M Anderson	12	217	-2
11	195	S Jackson	9	238	2
12	183	W Dunn	13	212	-1
13	171	W McGahee	16	199	-3
14	170	R Droughns	14	209	0
15	169	W Parker	18	187	-3
16	169	C Dillon	17	191	-1
17	165	D Davis	15	204	2
18	165	B Westbrook	11	226	7
19	158	C Williams	21	178	-2
20	157	C Brown	20	182	0

Figure 4.6

running backs deeper in the sense that they score more points once you leave the primary backs, but it still doesn't likely mean using a third-down back in your lineup will score nearly as well as an available wideout will.

There is another reality about running backs that must be considered when using reception points. They just do not catch the ball like they once did.

Figure 4.7 considers the top 40 scoring running backs using reception points for a 10-year period. The number of receptions peaked in 2002 and then has declined until an uptick at the top in 2006, thanks largely to Steven Jackson. The change was particularly felt by the top 20 backs while those ranked from 31st to 40th

NUMBER OF RECEPTIONS FOR THE TOP 40 RUNNING BACKS 1997–2006

Rank	1–10	11–20	21–30	31–40	Total
1997	371	317	327	236	1,251
1998	435	326	247	204	1,212
1999	501	323	356	332	1,512
2000	609	367	432	298	1,706
2001	601	378	367	217	1,563
2002	618	467	406	243	1,734
2003	548	458	363	230	1,599
2004	432	354	247	222	1,255
2005	389	314	250	294	1,247
2006	536	365	251	224	1,376

Figure 4.7

actually have been increasing. This has happened as a reflection of more use of a two-back system in the NFL, where one back is the primary receiving back and the other is the primary runner and scorer. This also happened because of the NFL rule change that required defenders to give receivers a five-yard buffer before contacting them and therefore allowed receivers to become better targets—especially the #2 and #3 wideouts for each team. Finally and perhaps every bit as significant, there are many more tight ends being used in passing now than ever before, and that comes at the expense of dump-off passes to running backs. Even more reason to think about changing a ranking based only on the addition of reception points.

Other than the rare running back like Westbrook who will have a high volume of passes compared to his running production, there is just no reason to adjust your rankings much for running backs when reception points are added. And while it does give more value to third-down backs who catch the ball, that is not as pronounced as the bump in value that is given to wideouts.

WIDE RECEIVERS

There is no single way to make wide receivers gain relative value more than reception points. These are the main players in the passing game and the ones who will enjoy higher scores than any other by virtue of catching the most passes. But do reception points translate into adjustments to your rankings of wideouts? As with running backs, there are some changes but nothing so significant to warrant a move of more than a couple of spots.

Using the same sample league, the results are a bit more noticeable with wideouts than running backs (see figure 4.8).

Now eight players have more than a two-position change and adjustments become more common deeper in the rankings. But before you let that set you off playing musical chairs with your wide-

CHANGE IN ACTUAL RESULTS WITHOUT AND WITH RECEPTION POINTS—WR'S

Rank	Without Rec Pts	Wideout	New Rank	With Rec Pts	Change in Rank
1	236	S Smith	1	339	0
2	203	L Fitzgerald	2	306	0
3	202	S Moss	6	286	-3
4	198	C Johnson	3	295	1
5	188	J Galloway	7	271	-2
6	187	T Holt	4	289	2
7	186	C Chambers	8	268	-1
8	186	M Harrison	9	268	-1
9	185	A Boldin	5	287	4
10	163	P Burress	10	239	0
11	163	H Ward	12	232	-1
12	161	T Glenn	15	223	-3
13	152	D Driver	11	238	2
14	147	T Houshmandzadeh	14	225	0
15	147	R Moss	21	207	-6
16	146	R Smith	13	231	3
17	145	K McCardell	17	215	0
18	144	E Kennison	18	212	0
19	138	J Smith	20	208	-1
20	135	D Stallworth	23	205	-3

Figure 4.8

out rankings, let's break down why there would be a significant change in how players scored when reception points are added.

1. **Touchdowns** Whenever players score a significantly higher number of touchdowns per catch than the rest of the league, they will become less valuable. But there are no wideouts who are reliably going to score a high amount of touchdowns compared to their number of catches. When it happens (such as with Joe Jurevicius when he was with the Seahawks), it is always an unforeseen event. This is not a factor to consider because it is an aberration for one year.

2. **Yards Per Catch** Those players that are at the top of the league in yards per catch will obviously fall back when reception points are introduced because they have proportionally fewer catches for their yardage than most receivers. This mainly applies to slot receivers and long-ball specialists who will not normally rate as a fantasy team starter but can apply to a few of the top wideouts. Think of speedsters like Santana Moss for those rare exceptions and drop them in your rankings.

3. **Possession Receivers** These are the players that benefit the most by adding reception points to the scoring equation. You can feel safe moving a known possession receiver up a few spots in your rankings. These are the players like Anquan Boldin, Chris Chambers, Donald Driver, and so on who may not have a lot of touchdowns. They may not have a high average yards per catch. But they get the number of catches to give them greater consistency with higher scoring each week—and reliably so.

CHANGE IN ACTUAL RESULTS WITHOUT AND WITH RECEPTION POINTS—TE'S

Rank	Without Rec Pts	Tight End	New Rank	With Rec Pts	Change in Rank
1	170	A Gates	1	259	0
2	131	J Shockey	3	196	-1
3	126	T Heap	2	201	1
4	118	C Cooley	4	189	0
5	117	A Crumpler	5	182	0
6	110	J Witten	7	176	-1
7	102	T Gonzalez	6	180	1
8	88	R McMichael	8	148	0
9	85	L Smith	9	146	0
10	85	J Stevens	10	130	0
11	81	H Miller	13	120	-2
12	75	B Troupe	11	130	1

Figure 4.9

Compared to other positions, wide receivers get the biggest boost from reception points, and while they do make more rankings changes than seen in any other position, it still is not a huge difference. Just push those possession receivers up a couple of slots and downgrade the players with a high average yards per catch and call it good.

TIGHT ENDS

The addition of reception points instantly made tight ends a factor in weekly scoring, but as with all things tight end, there is nothing more to consider than those top 12 players (see figure 4.9).

Within the position, the change is virtually nonexistent. In our sample league, only one player moved two spots thanks to a higher number of touchdowns per catch than most, while half of the top 12 had no change with reception points added. The other five shifted only one spot—that is not nearly enough to consider tight end rankings any differently with or without reception points. They score better with the receptions, but within the position—just leave your rankings intact.

Reception points have great benefits to a fantasy league in making drafts go deeper with valuable players and a far more diverse selection of positions in the early rounds. They make the league more competitive and offer the fantasy team owners at The Next Level more ways to win. And yet—they really do not change how the players fall in rankings. It's all win and no loss with reception points. And it is the #1 way to recharge an existing league.

SECTION

II

THE **Preseason**

CREATING YOUR OWN
PROJECTIONS

5

*With many calculations, one can win; with few one cannot.
How much less chance of victory has one who makes none
at all!*

(Sun Tzu, The Art of War*)*

THE BASIS FOR ALL FANTASY SPORTS is the accumulation
of statistics that are used in awarding fantasy points based on performance. It only stands to reason that you must understand how
those statistics are created and what the most reasonable projection
of them is for the upcoming season. As the rule says, *draft your team
for this year and not from last year.* This means focusing on prior stats
only to help you determine what this year will likely bring. The
average fantasy player does not bother to project stats for players;
but the process is not only enjoyable, it helps you become far more
knowledgeable about the one thing that matters most—the upcoming season. Last year happened and will never happen again. While
it may seem like a lot of work, it's nothing more than you likely do
during the season when you determine which of your players you
want to start. You look at his past, you consider his present, and
you forecast his future. There are certainly many more players to
consider than the few eventually on your team, but you have the
summer to work on it and it's the single best way to understand the
NFL as it applies to fantasy football.

The process of creating player projections yields several pro-
foundly significant benefits to anyone playing fantasy football.

1. **Removing Bias** While we all want to believe that we are objective, the reality is that all fantasy team owners are also fans of the NFL in the first place. That means there are at least predispositions for and against certain players and teams. Projecting out hard numbers based on historical data and current situations removes the tendency to draft players that you like over others that will do more for your team—like 'em or not.

2. **Learning the True Value of Players** Projecting players will yield a familiarity with what every player has done and will most likely do in the one category that matters most—statistics. It allows you to become much more knowledgeable about the recent history of players beyond those flashy film clips on *SportsCenter*. In many ways, the NFL is an entertainment sport. In all ways, fantasy football is a statistical pursuit.

3. **Setting Up Customized Rankings** A LAG analysis will show that not all leagues value players equally. A player will be more valuable in one league than another depending upon the fantasy scoring rules, and that, of course, stems directly from the statistics he is most likely to generate. That can be translated into fantasy points unique to your league.

There is no way to be serious and consistently successful in fantasy football without projecting players yourself. Preparing for your fantasy season without projecting statistics is like an NFL team spending their off-season training without an actual football. Statistics are THE thing. So is the football. Nothing else matters as much.

So how should you project performances for a season? Just grab the stats from last year and tweak here and there? Sure—that would be better than nothing. Not a lot more, but better than nothing. The reality of projecting performances is that the only true constant in the NFL is "change." This leads us to our next rule:

Rule 5

Teams change every year, even when they don't.

The NFL is in a constant state of flux. There are numerous differences from season to season with coaching and staffing replacements, new offensive schemes, and a normal turnover rate for depth charts. This is why merely tweaking the previous numbers usually produces a less accurate result.

Consider a sample quarterback who comes back the next year with the same coaches and players—he should just repeat his last year's numbers, right? Sir Isaac Newton actually shed a little light on that thought:

> *An object at rest tends to stay at rest and an object in motion tends to stay in motion with the same speed and same direction unless acted upon by an external force.*

Assuming that the sample quarterback will repeat his previous season is ignoring the law above. Yes, it would be reasonable to assume the object (quarterback) would continue with the same speed and direction (production) if in fact he traveled in a time machine to the previous season or he played in a vacuum where everyone followed a script. This is why fantasy professional wrestling has never caught on. The most important part of Newton's law is *"unless acted upon by an external force."* In this case, therein lies all the difference.

Even with the same coaches, scheme, and receivers, the reality is that he will not be playing the exact same schedule against unchanged teams. What about the effect of his running game? Will his offensive line perform better or worse? Have his opposing defenses improved? Since everyone is a year older, is it reasonable to expect the same level of health from all players on the team? Will opponents have new coaches and offensive/defensive schemes to consider?

In the rare event that a team shows up the next season without any changes of apparent consequence, the reality is that it still is a different team because the schedule will be different, the players are one year older, and the opponents will not be exactly as they were the previous year. Fantasy points are not gained by players in May wearing shorts during an inter-squad practice. They are gained against an opponent that has worked on their weaknesses and tried to hold on to their strengths. Teams change if only because they will face opponents that will be different this year. Bank on it.

This makes projecting players more of an art than a science. Final rankings should never be "generated" as if some computerized process could merely take input data, perform calculations, and spit out "the way things will be." Many of the variables to consider are not quantifiable and are not conducive to being turned into a number value despite being perhaps the most important success factors. There are many in the fantasy community who want to believe that projections are merely a function of pushing *Enter* on a keyboard, but our next rule is perhaps the greatest truth of them all:

Rule 6

There is nothing as important as having
a genuine feel for the game.

It is only by understanding the game, generally over many seasons, that a person can embrace what the NFL has been, is, and will be like. If projections could be had by merely pushing *Enter*, we might as well all follow corporate America's lead and farm out the cheat sheets to India while we go play golf. This is not to discourage the new fantasy player or to take a swat at some casual veteran. It is merely a dose of reality. Projecting players is critical to understanding the NFL and what to expect, which then feeds all you will do in a fantasy football draft and later managing your team. The better your projections are, the better your rankings will be. And the better your team will be. And so on.

USING PAST STATISTICS AS A GUIDELINE

While never the only guide, the use of previous statistics by a player is an obvious first step to be used in determining his most likely performance for the upcoming season. Fantasy football is a statistical game and knowing what a player has done has tremendous bearing on what to expect for the next season. As stated before, if all you did was to take the previous year's numbers and tweak them, you'd be far better off than others who just grab a convenient cheat sheet and then select players based on personal preferences. But you would not be at The Next Level.

There are three critical steps involved in analyzing players, which bring to light a far better picture of what performance can reasonably be expected:

1. Review and project players the same as you should value them—team first, position second, and individual last.

2. Analyze and understand the last three years of a player's history, not just the previous season and not just an average.

3. Review the per game statistics gained by a player for the previous season to determine trends and consistency.

TEAM FIRST

If there is one single aspect of a fantasy team owner that signifies The Next Level, it is that he or she understands the importance of the team to each player. The NFL is not tennis or golf where players perform independently from everyone else. Everything that a football player does is within the context of the team—how he fits into the scheme, his role, and the offense around him. This is precisely why projecting players independently makes little sense and yields even less accurate results.

While players will have greatly differing performances in any given season, the reality is that the actual difference between players is far smaller than is commonly recognized. That is not to say there are not some players who are truly gifted but through the never-ending culling process that leads to the NFL, only the best athletes in the country end up playing professional football. There are roughly 120 Division I-A, 120 Division I-AA, 140 Division II, and 230 Division III schools that have football programs. That means there are well over 600 starting college quarterbacks in the country that can opt to turn pro in any given year. And yet typically fewer than 16 are actually drafted and most of those end up as little more than camp arms.

This means only around one in every 40 college quarterbacks makes it to the NFL, and even in Division 1-A, only about one in every 10 gets drafted. Each draft class eventually produces only about three or four quarterbacks who become starters of any note in the NFL. This means that just one out of every 200 starting college quarterbacks becomes an NFL starter for any period of time. We like to ridicule certain quarterbacks for having no talent, but the reality is that they were more talented than 99.5 percent of all other college quarterbacks by becoming NFL starters. The same ratios hold for other positions as well.

By no means is this to suggest that all players are interchangeable, but it does demonstrate that players entering the NFL are already very athletic, experienced, and talented. How many times have you seen either high school or even college stars flop at the highest level, if they even make it that far? What matters most to these incoming rookies and the veterans in the NFL is that they get the opportunity to play in a scheme that favors them for a team with the ability to have success with that offense. Guaranteed—there are hundreds of players in the NFL who would shine given the right opportunity, scheme, and team dynamics. This is why players experience a "magic year" when everything comes together for them even if it only happens once in a career. This is why players changing teams sometimes experience vastly differing production.

The point is that you cannot evaluate or project for a player independent of their team. Remember—team first. There is no "I" in team and there is no "wild ass guessing" in winning a championship. The scheme—and all the players that contribute to it—must be considered in order to evaluate a player's likely output for the next season. All the components of an offense have to work together for success. An offense is like a symphony that is trying to play from the middle of a mosh pit. How each position relates to their team will be considered in positional breakdowns to follow, but remember at all times what you were taught on your first day of football practice:

Team First.

USING THREE YEARS OF STATISTICS

The player statistics from the most recent season are obviously of interest but they only tell one story—the unique situation they were in the previous season: their teammates, schedule, health, and

COMPARISON OF 4 SAMPLE RUNNING BACKS FROM THE PREVIOUS YEAR

Player	1	2	3	4
Year	3	3	3	3
Team	A	B	C	D
Games	16	11	12	16
Runs	337	209	220	352
Rush Yards	1,458	733	735	1,516
YPC	4.3	3.5	3.3	4.3
Rush TD's	12	12	5	11
Targets	30	25	31	41
Catches	23	22	24	30
Catch Yards	90	181	118	216
Catch TD's	0	1	0	0

Figure 5.1

a host of other variables. By reviewing the most recent three years for a player, their consistency and trends are much more apparent. Consider the sample statistics for four different running backs during one season (see figure 5.1).

Here, Players 1 and 4 look like rock-solid running backs while both Players 2 and 3 would be considered just backups, other than the unusually high number of touchdowns scored by Player 2. Both Players 2 and 3 missed some games, so maybe they should have higher projections for this year? Let's take a three-year look at these players for a more complete picture of their statistics (see figure 5.2).

3-YEAR STATS FOR RUNNING BACK #1

Player	1	1	1
Year	1	2	3
Team	A	A	A
Games	13	16	16
Runs	214	362	337
Rush Yards	967	1,457	1,458
YPC	4.5	4.0	4.3
Rush TD's	9	12	12
Targets	23	26	30
Catches	21	15	23
Catch Yards	146	84	90
Catch TD's	0	0	0

Figure 5.2

Player 1 comes off a great season and, judging by the numbers here, he's been consistently productive the last three years and the last two seasons were almost identical. His initial projection has to be considered to be a replication of the past season unless some aspect has changed for him this season. His numbers may be tempered by the dynamics of the team around him and even the schedule he will face, but until those are determined this player looks due for a repeat.

Player 2 was the oddity who had barely moderate yardage but scored 13 times the previous season. Considering his three-year picture, more questions than answers arise. He changed teams and

3-YEAR STATS FOR RUNNING BACK #2

Player	2	2	2
Year	1	2	3
Team	E	B	B
Games	13	15	11
Runs	138	345	209
Rush Yards	541	1,635	733
YPC	3.9	4.7	3.5
Rush TD's	2	12	12
Targets	17	19	25
Catches	11	15	22
Catch Yards	71	103	181
Catch TD's	0	1	1

Figure 5.3

had a very nice season (1,738 yards and 13 touchdowns) but while he maintained his 13 scores in the third year, his rushing yardage diminished by more than half and his yards per carry dropped well below the four-yard NFL standard despite being a lofty 4.7 the previous season. He also has not played a full 16 games in the last three years. This looks like an older player who may have witnessed a magic year but is battling durability issues each season. While much more research is needed to determine a realistic projection, the only certainty is that just replicating the previous year is meaningless with this player.

Player 3 has the same yardage as Player 2 last year, but his numbers prompt fewer questions. His production was down in year

3-YEAR STATS FOR RUNNING BACK #3

Player	3	3	3
Year	1	2	3
Team	C	C	C
Games	16	16	12
Runs	321	371	220
Rush Yards	1,311	1,697	735
YPC	4.1	4.6	3.3
Rush TD's	2	12	5
Targets	51	47	31
Catches	42	41	24
Catch Yards	262	245	118
Catch TD's	0	2	0

Figure 5.4

three but he missed four games and, judging by his yards per carry, it appears he was likely playing injured for an extended part of the season. His year two scores were dramatically better than the other seasons. The two main decisions that demand research here are determining why his yards per carry were so low and factoring in why his year two touchdowns were so high. This initially looks like a running back who had one big year followed by one bad year with an injury. With no change in which team he plays for, his year one numbers are likely the best starting projection for this player with a bit higher touchdowns.

Player 4 was the other highly productive running back, and his three-year look tells a favorable story. After a very nice year

3-YEAR STATS FOR RUNNING BACK #4

Player	4	4	4
Year	1	2	3
Team	F	D	D
Games	13	15	16
Runs	290	343	352
Rush Yards	1,591	1,315	1,516
YPC	5.5	3.8	4.3
Rush TD's	14	5	11
Targets	55	60	41
Catches	38	40	30
Catch Yards	314	235	216
Catch TD's	0	2	0

Figure 5.5

one with a different team that even saw him miss three games, he switched to a new club and had a down year in scores and yardage. In his third season (second with the new team), he returned to his previous form of year one with a decrease in yards per carry but still healthy with a 4.3 average. Until changed by other variables yet considered, his initial projection should be around what he had done the previous season if not slightly higher from entering his third year in the same scheme.

For demonstration purposes, we reviewed four sample running backs, but remember that this level of analysis should be conducted per team, not by position. Placing the three-year statistics for all players on the same team allows you to reach The Next Level in determining the most reasonable projections for a player, and many of the variables to be considered later will be the same for all players on that team. Projecting by team not only yields superior results, it also is an easier way to work.

PER GAME STATISTICS

After reviewing the last three seasons for a player and establishing an initial projection, the next step is digging a bit more into the statistics that the player generated in each game of the prior year. Total numbers are fine in a fantasy league that is a "total points" league, but most use weekly head-to-head match-ups to tally wins. We need to investigate how those totals from last year came about since that also plays directly into what the player's projections will be for the upcoming season. Consider three sample wideouts who ended with similar fantasy points for the past year.

All three players produced very similar overall statistics and, considering just total numbers, it appears that these three wideouts would be interchangeable. The next step in projections—reviewing those per game stats—shows a much different picture, which plays directly into his projections for this year.

COMPARISON OF 3 SAMPLE WIDEOUTS: PREVIOUS YEAR						
Player	Fantasy Points	Games Played	Thrown to	Catches	Yards	TD's
A	147	14	118	78	1,112	8
B	147	16	124	60	1,005	8
C	145	16	107	70	917	9

Figure 5.6

PER GAME BREAKDOWN FOR SAMPLE WIDEOUTS

Player A				Player B				Player C			
Week	Catches	Yards	TD's	Week	Catches	Yards	TD's	Week	Catches	Yards	TD's
1	Did Not Play			1	2	18		1	9	123	2
2	Did Not Play			2	5	86		2	5	73	
3	3	59	1	3	1	7	1	3	7	58	1
4	5	75		4	3	26		4	3	88	1
5	5	55	1	5	1	28	1	5	4	80	2
6	8	105		6	0	0		6	6	58	
7	5	88	2	7	3	40		7	6	88	1
8	7	75		8	5	72		8	5	78	1
9	5	77	1	9	3	43	1	9	6	51	
10	5	61		10	7	74		10	1	5	
11	5	47		11	6	87	1	11	2	20	
12	9	147	1	12	5	130	1	12	4	54	
13	6	53	1	13	5	127	1	13	2	25	
14	7	70		14	4	123		14	5	45	
15	6	61	1	15	7	116	2	15	1	11	1
16	2	43		16	3	28		16	4	60	

Figure 5.7

Player A   Breaking down his statistics per game reveals a very consistent performer who would have had better numbers had he played those first two games. With such a nice spacing out of yardage and scores, he looks like a lock to perform at the same level this season unless changes around him demand tweaking. He only had two games over 100 yards but was always solid on yardage, even throwing a score in as well every other week or so. Looks like a solid player with similar projections from last year at this point.

Player B Though this player ended last year with numbers similar to the other two players, this is the guy I would most want to own and who obviously should be considered for a healthy bump in projections this coming year over what he did in the last season. After a slow start, he caught fire by midseason and then ended the year on a tremendous, "championship-winning" roll. You need to determine if some temporary dynamic was at play last year but this looks like a classic breakout player.

Player C Started the year with a big bang and by midseason he already had eight touchdowns. But he only scored once more the rest of the year, never had a game over 100 yards, and apparently just disappeared later on when you would have needed him most. Obviously you have to determine if there was an injury involved; but otherwise this player either enjoyed very uncharacteristic success catching touchdowns early in the year or some team dynamic changed and absolutely bit him in the ass. His projections are not only to be lowered but this has the look of a player who someone else will value far more than me in my drafts.

These are three players who all had similar total numbers in the previous season, but the per game investigation reveals that we are really dealing with a trio of wide receivers who will fall into three different tiers and should have dramatically more separation in their production this year than last. While the example only uses sample players, the reality is that the more knowledge you acquire, the more readily you can decipher what happened the previous season.

There is one other qualifier when you are reviewing per game statistics. It is obviously important to see the number of big games that a player had in the previous season. *It is also important to con-*

sider against whom those numbers were produced. If all the big games came against weak defenses from nondivisional rivals who they will not play again, devalue them a bit, if not a lot. Similarly, if a player was turning in nice fantasy numbers against divisional rivals that he will be facing twice every season, then even more value should be given to those games.

In the event you do not have immediate access to the statistics, check to see if your league uses either a desktop or Internet league management tool, since it is likely the statistics can be lifted from that source. They are also available in some form at most large football sites and are available for free at TheHuddle.com.

Each NFL player will either improve, stay the same, or decline with each new season, and using a two-step approach to initial projections—three-year first and then per game of the last year—is a great tool for deciding which direction he is likely headed and just how different next year should be. This is crucial because projections feed your rankings/cheat sheet, which builds your team, which decides your fate. While projecting out the entire league has its benefits, you needn't take it to that level. At the minimum, do your projections for any player who you believe will likely be worthy of being a fantasy starter and perhaps one level of fantasy backups for running backs. In a standard league of 12 teams that starts QB, 2 RB, 3 WR, and TE, you should at least do around 18 quarterbacks, 36 running backs, 36 wide receivers, and a dozen tight ends.

Don't let the task seem daunting—it isn't. And the more you project players, the more you know and the easier and faster it becomes.

QUARTERBACKS

"The most important thing to remember is to protect your quarterback—ME!"

(From The Longest Yard, *1974)*

AFTER HAVING MADE INITIAL PROJECTIONS considering three-year and per game statistics, the next step is to dive into those areas and characteristics that are largely unquantifiable. They have a direct and profound bearing upon the current and future value of a player but they do not come with nifty numerical expressions. In short—you have to work to understand them. And in reality—they make all the difference.

Coming fresh off our statistical discussion and still in a mathematical mind set, here is the conceptual equation for determining a player's production:

$$Player\ Value\ =\ Talent\ \times\ Situation\ \times\ Opportunity$$

This is an absolute truth. Each player enters the season with some amount of talent, which will be used as often as the opportunity presents itself, and the success will be in some measure dependent upon the situation that he is playing within. All three criteria are essential for success. A player with no talent (insert your most hated player here) will not succeed. This is mostly why I am writing this and you are reading it instead of me throwing touchdown passes to you in the Super Bowl. We're not nearly talented enough to succeed (or likely stay alive) on the football field.

Players who have great talent and belong to a team that presents a great situation are likewise meaningless if a player's involvement is limited to wearing a cap sideways while sitting on the bench. They have to play in order to post numbers. While this may seem screamingly obvious, remember this the next time you want to burn an earlier draft pick on a player that "may" get a starting job.

Lastly, situation is an equally significant criterion. The team must have the personnel to execute an effective scheme that will use a player in the way that best produces good statistics. How many times have you heard "anyone could do well in that system"? Or better yet, how many teams have become an NFL Siberia—swallowing up talented players and crushing what they could have done on a good team? A talented running back who carries the ball 350 times a year will never approach his true potential if his line couldn't block a troop of Girl Scouts selling cookies. The most talented tight end in the world is worthless if his quarterback has the nasty habit of just throwing the ball away on most plays. Or if the tight end is merely a blocker by design.

Talent, opportunity, and situation—these are the three areas that define a player's value and control what statistics he will be able to produce. That remains as the basic tenet of evaluating and analyzing players. However, reaching The Next Level means realizing that all positions are not equal and that the three criteria, while vital for every player, vary in importance according to position. Talent, opportunity, and situation are the key to any player, but you have to shape the key to fit the particular lock. Consider the quarterback production value equation:

Rule 7

QB Value = Talent × (Situation × 2) × Opportunity

What this abstract equation states is that talent and opportunity are very important—equally so. A quarterback must have the opportunity to be on the field (a given) and be talented enough to successfully execute the plays that are called. But more important in producing big statistics is how often he is asked to run those passing plays, the quality of the receivers, and how well the scheme addresses the defense each week. And just as important, how well his blockers are giving him time to throw the ball to receivers who can get open and actually catch the pass. The components of a passing play are quite complex and unless all facets work well and productive pass plays are called, the quarterback will not post big numbers regardless if his team wins the game.

Recall a player like Troy Aikman. This vastly talented quarterback and first overall pick in the 1989 draft went to the Cowboys. He was a starter for 12 years but he only once threw more than 19 touchdowns in any season despite winning three Super Bowls. His situation was that the Cowboys had a great defense and a deadly rushing game with Emmitt Smith, and Aikman was rarely called on to pass extensively. He did have a game where he passed for five touchdowns. He once threw for 455 yards in a single game. He just did not play within a scheme that called on him to throw much or rely on the pass for touchdowns that often. Talent? Absolutely—first overall pick in 1989 and later a Hall of Famer. Opportunity? He played in 165 games. Situation? Say hello to a fantasy dud (okay, so maybe he was a decent fantasy backup).

In analyzing the value of a quarterback, the most important characteristic is his situation. He must have decent blocking on passing plays and have them called often to produce notable statistics. And he must have a cast of receivers that can turn a pass into a long play or even a touchdown. Objectively, which quarterback do you think will have the most fantasy value—a super-talented one who rarely throws or the moderately talented player who is either in an offensive scheme that prefers the pass or on a team that often finds itself in a *situation* where it must constantly throw to catch up on the scoreboard? Give that moderately talented guy at least one or two decent receivers and he'll post the better numbers.

Each quarterback's talent, opportunity, and especially situation are what produce those statistics that fantasy fanatics love to pore over. They are the driving forces behind the numbers he will produce and—since his talent and opportunity are already proven—the next step to tweaking his projections is to consider his situation for the upcoming season. All things being equal, the most talented quarterback would naturally post the best numbers. But nothing is equal, and the situation is why.

CONCERNS AND ADJUSTMENTS

Each season ushers in at least minimal changes for every team and those must be factored regarding the future value of a quarterback.

1. **Coaching Changes** Any change to the staff will have an effect: most notably the head coach, offensive coordinator, and even potentially a quarterbacks coach or offensive line coach. Even a change in defensive coordinators can impact the quarterback if it involves installing a new scheme, which naturally will take time to work and will likely lead to worse starting field positions if not more games in which the team is close or trailing. Is the offensive scheme well known and poised to execute plays well?

2. **Offensive Line** Pass blocking may not be as intricate as rush blocking but it still has critical facets to consider. Is it reasonable to assume that the line will be able to pick up blitzes reasonably well? And if the

offensive line is not at least average, is the quarterback mobile enough to buy time with his feet when needed? How reliable is the left tackle, who must prevent the blindside sacks?

3. **Health Issues** Every season, there are usually only about 14 quarterbacks who actually play a full 16-game season. Most only miss one or two games and a couple might sit out the last week on purpose. But quarterbacks do get hurt often if only because every defensive lineman is trying to get a highlight clip on every play. Consider the health history of the quarterback as well as his protection.

4. **Rushing Game** The better the rushing game, the less need for passing. Every team will run first if there is an option since an effective ground game controls the ball and eats the clock. It also minimizes the risks that come with passing—sacks, fumbles, and interceptions. Is there a reason to believe that the team will run better in the new season? A new running back perhaps?

5. **Receivers** Obviously the quality of the receivers is critical for the success of a quarterback, but do not diminish the value of all receivers—wideouts, tight ends, and running backs. History is the best indicator, particularly the longer the set of receivers have played together and in the same scheme.

6. **Scheme** Simple enough—has history shown this offense to prefer to pass more or to run more? There are only a handful of teams that heavily prefer the pass (traditionally the Colts and Rams) and then there are teams that have crappy running games and have no

choice but to throw the ball. And lastly, teams that chronically trail in games are going to throw more often as well. Bottom line here—how much is the team likely to pass the ball and how well versed are the personnel in that scheme?

7. **Schedule**   The schedule impacts every team, but differently when considering quarterbacks. A review of the schedule will show how likely a team will be throwing out of need instead of mere desire. A bad schedule actually helps a quarterback unless it includes facing top-notch cornerbacks and safeties.

Each quarterback will be performing within the dynamics of his team against a slate of opponents. That must be considered in projecting and valuing a quarterback for the coming season. Initial projections should be largely based on historical statistics but that should only be a starting point. All of the above seven characteristics should be factored into your projections for any quarterback.

STUD REPEATABILITY

Everyone loves a stud. Having the highest-scoring quarterback is obviously an advantage when you roll up all your starter scores every week. Many and perhaps most casual fantasy drafters use the previous season as the main template for ranking players, but those at The Next Level recognize just how fickle that thought process can be. Consider how quarterbacks over a 10-year period have fared from season to season. This is using a standard fantasy scoring but would hold true in almost any scoring scenario.

WHERE TOP 5 QUARTERBACKS FINISHED THEIR NEXT SEASON

Ended	Top 5	6th–10th	11th–20th	>20th
1997	3	1	0	1
1998	1	0	2	2
1999	1	1	0	3
2000	2	1	1	1
2001	2	2	1	0
2002	1	3	0	1
2003	2	0	1	2
2004	3	1	1	0
2005	1	1	2	1
2006	3	1	1	0

Figure 6.1

What this chart says is that a top five quarterback almost always has less than a 50 percent chance of repeating the next season. Removing the obvious players such as Brett Favre (early years), Peyton Manning, and Daunte Culpepper (until 2005), almost no quarterbacks who end up top five one year will be there again the following season. More than anything, this shows that other than Peyton Manning, there is almost no reason to expect a quarterback to make the top five in consecutive seasons.

The good news here is that taking a top five quarterback usually results in a starting quality player—just do not pay too dearly for him since there is a good chance he will drop to being solid instead of spectacular.

WHERE 6TH TO 11TH BEST QUARTERBACKS FINISHED THEIR NEXT SEASON

Ended	Top 5	6th–10th	11th–20th	>20th
1997	0	1	2	2
1998	1	0	2	2
1999	0	1	2	2
2000	0	2	2	1
2001	0	1	2	2
2002	1	0	2	2
2003	1	3	1	0
2004	0	2	0	3
2005	1	0	4	0
2006	1	0	1	3

Figure 6.2

What this chart says is that a quarterback who ended in the sixth to 10th best range one year had almost no chance of improving dramatically. Only four times in 10 years (50 possible chances) did such a quarterback rise to become a top five player. Those four players (Steve Young, Rich Gannon, Trent Green, and Michael Vick) were not just bouncing back and forth either. They were four different players, and in the cases of Young and Gannon, both had no fantasy value the following year.

What this chart shows more than anything is the changing nature of the position and how there is even less reliability in quarterbacks now than in previous years. Up until 2002, the numbers were incredibly consistent. Since that time, no more than one second-tier quarterback rose up to become a top five player. This is significant because a top five player is a true difference-maker. Anything less is only average at best in a fantasy league of 10 or 12 team owners.

WHERE SLEEPERS COME FROM

The best situation for a fantasy owner is to draft a quarterback with a later pick who ends up as a top five player. It allows a fantasy team to stock up on other positions with coveted players and not pay any price for waiting on a quarterback. Consider how top five quarterbacks performed in the season prior to their breakout year (see figure 6.3).

WHERE QUARTERBACKS FINISHED THE PREVIOUS SEASON BEFORE A TOP 5 YEAR				
Ended	Top 5	6th–10th	11th–20th	>20th
1997	3	0	0	2
1998	1	1	1	2
1999	1	0	2	2
2000	2	0	1	2
2001	2	0	2	1
2002	1	1	1	2
2003	2	1	1	1
2004	3	0	2	0
2005	1	1	2	1
2006	3	1	0	1

Figure 6.3

As we discovered previously, those players ending in the sixth to 10th tier one year were not very likely to end up as a top five pick. Historically, there are usually two in the top five who were not even in the top 20 the previous season (though that has started to change).

There is a definite trend with those top five sleeper quarterbacks (see Appendix, Table I). They invariably fall into one of two categories. Either they are a quarterback who has been successful with a previous team but for whatever reason is replaced (Jeff George, Brad Johnson, and Drew Bledsoe) and lands on a team with veteran receivers and a scheme that used the pass heavily. If not, the best bet is that the sleeper was a quarterback who only played one previous season for about half the games and then became the opening day starter in his second or third season. Those sleepers—the guys you could draft cheap and laugh maniacally about by the end of the year—were almost all in the first season as a starter with their team.

BREAKOUT YEARS

Sleepers can also be defined as a player having a "breakout" season, where their production not only takes a significant jump upward, but it is also enough to land him in the top five for the season. Those best five quarterbacks each season are truly the difference-makers, and managing to grab one using a deeper pick in your draft is like buying a cheap pair of glasses that claim to allow you to see through clothing and then discovering that they actually work.

"Uh yeah, I expected that all along . . . ahem . . . Looking good, Susie . . ."

The importance of finding a player who is due for a breakout season is not that you should crave taking a risk—and he will be, regardless—it is that these players invariably are undervalued in drafts. A winning draft means taking players that perform at least at a level commensurate with where you drafted them and preferably at a level much higher. Same goes for auction drafts where limited dollars are chasing a pool of players and you must extract more value than what you paid.

Certainly any quarterback has the potential of a breakout season given the right mixture of talent, situation, and opportunity, but there are some consistent trends (see Appendix, Table II). The majority of breakout quarterbacks shot up in their second or third season in the NFL—usually their first season as a true starter. There are also a number of first-round picks who played in the end of their rookie season and waited only after a year of seasoning to deliver on that pricey rookie contract. But generally, quarterbacks usually take a season or two before their talent can adjust to the level of play in the NFL, and once that happens breakout years occur.

There are exceptions to this rule. Players like Trent Green and Rich Gannon had banged around the league until finding the right situation, which is almost impossible to forecast. They were veterans who had only played a handful of full seasons and ended up breaking out in their first or second season with a new team. Also outside the norm were Steve McNair and Jake Plummer, who had played many years before finally turning in a truly big year. McNair had been flirting with it for many seasons and finally nudged into the top tier. Plummer switched teams in order to find his optimal situation (aka "anywhere but Arizona").

ROOKIES

While there are great reasons to consider rookies for other positions, quarterback is absolutely, positively not one of them. Yes, Peyton Manning did end up around a top five quarterback as a rookie (if you were not penalized for interceptions) but there are usually around 14 quarterbacks drafted every season. So for 10 years, not drafting a rookie quarterback as your fantasy starter meant you were right in about 139 out of 140 cases.

Just say no. Please.

DRAFTING PLANS

First and foremost, understand your league using a LAG analysis to see how quarterbacks are valued in your league and how they best fit into your draft plans. Create your initial projections based on statistical considerations and then adjust them using the seven criteria previously described. What you most likely will conclude is that taking a quarterback early in the draft does not make much sense unless he is (currently) Peyton Manning. The repeatability is not there to rely on and the variation in how quarterbacks rise and fall has been getting less consistent as time passes.

Despite this, a quarterback is probably your highest-scoring player or close to it. But that doesn't mean getting one with a very early pick since you only start one and, as such, everyone starts just one. That means that quality exists for a starting quality quarterback well into the middle rounds of almost any draft.

Sleeper quarterbacks can be had very cheaply and, as shown above, there are some common keys to consider to determine who you should secretly covet in a draft. The sleeper stars have almost always been first-year starters for their team, whether that was after a year of playing only part of the season, or switching teams with a chip on their shoulder, making him ripe for at least one season of big numbers before defenses had enough game film to know how to stop him. That matters greatly in how a quarterback performs and is the reason why quarterbacks changing teams can turn in a huge initial season and then quickly fade away.

Bottom line—quarterbacks are likely one of your highest scorers, but you only need one of them. Unless scoring is slanted to the advantage of the passer, chances are high that your fantasy drafts will yield great value in quarterbacks even as deeply as mid-draft—later for that backup quarterback who should strategically be selected as a sleeper candidate.

RUNNING BACKS

7

"Ability is nothing without opportunity."

THERE ARE RUNNING BACKS. There are non–running backs. This is basically how most fantasy football fans differentiate NFL players. There is no doubt that owning two top running backs—if even possible—grants a big advantage in almost every league out there. Not only do they score more than any other position (or close), they are the most consistent player on your roster. Other than perhaps two or three teams each season, every NFL offense is predicated on establishing a ground game. The reasons are valid—control the clock and tempo of the game, keep the opposing offense off the field and yet minimize the chance that the defense is going to take the ball away from them. Nothing is worse than throwing an end zone interception. A one-yard plunge for a score will make any head coach smile.

In fantasy terms, the running backs are the foundation of your team. High-scoring and consistent, they will be running up your weekly score better and more often than any other player outside possibly a super-stud quarterback or wideout. Because of this reality, it doesn't take very long for all league mates to recognize how valuable running backs can be. Anyone who has been in a league with knowledgeable owners has likely witnessed drafts where the first and possibly even the second rounds were slanted almost exclusively toward running backs.

Since they are so important and coveted, getting your running back choices correct is critical. Get them right and your team becomes solid with only a sleeper or two from other positions needed to secure that championship. Get them wrong or wait too long on them and reaching the playoffs too often becomes a nightmare of team management and waiver wire scrounging. While quarterbacks need a great situation to shine, that is not the most important criterion for running backs because almost all NFL teams desperately crave a sound running game. Let's differentiate running backs from quarterbacks in this way:

Rule 8

RB Value = Talent × Situation × (Opportunity × 2)

In the NFL draft, teams are searching for the most talented running back—that does not necessarily carry over to your fantasy draft. Sure, having a super-talent like Shaun Alexander or LaDainian Tomlinson makes a running game better, without a doubt, but in this day and age of Running-Back-by-Committee (RBBC) and specialists for short yardage, third down, and the goal line, it is the opportunity that each back gets that most determines his fantasy value.

The best fantasy back usually does not have the highest yards per carry of any running back. It will be healthy, no doubt, but it typically is not the highest. The best running backs are the ones that are getting between 330 and 370 carries a season (20+ per game) with a healthy dose of touchdowns because they take the goal line duty as well. Running back is as close as a "plug and play" player as you can find on an NFL team (okay, plus the kicker). Is this fantasy heresy? Not at all. Consider that no offensive ball-handling position witnesses as much success with inexperienced rookies than a running back.

Consider the dynamics of a pass play. The center has to sometimes make a shotgun snap and the offensive line has to block between four and eight defenders who are making a beeline for the quarterback's rib cage. The quarterback has to make his reads on a play, while sensing if his life is in immediate danger, and typically will scan through two or three receivers on most plays. Only rarely is a play a lock to go to one player. He must find the receiver running the correct pattern and without coverage that removes him as an option. As the ball is zipping through the air toward the receivers, so is the nearby secondary, who first wants to intercept the ball and secondly wants to force an incompletion, and if all that fails, the defensive back wants to leave the receiver in a crumpled mass on the field.

Conversely, a running play has the quarterback taking a safe, direct snap and then handing off to a running back who already knows exactly where he is to run. The offensive linemen are all blocking to create and maintain that hole. Either the tailback runs through it and then gets as far as he can or he sees that it is closed and improvises in another direction. The primary success factor is how well the offensive line opens that running lane—not how many times the running back was in Heisman contention.

Every season witnesses at least one or two big surprises from previously unknown players becoming a starting tailback. Does that player's success automatically anoint him as a starter the next season? Of course not, at least not in all cases. It is a running back. It is more opportunity and situation than talent that posts fantasy points for tailbacks. The most talented running backs are saddled with greater focus by the defenses while middle-tier or replacement backs are fortunate enough not to face eight players on every run. When you evaluate running backs, the first key is what his opportunity will be that season. As de facto talent evaluators, fantasy fans naturally love the most talented running backs but the more questions there are about the opportunity a back will receive, the less attractive he is in a fantasy draft.

CONCERNS AND ADJUSTMENTS

Running backs are the most consistent performers and even year to year they still do better than other positions overall in repeating their previous performance. Let's look at the reasons your projections and attitude toward a player should be reconsidered:

1. **Coaching Changes**   Fortunately, most running backs are insulated from negative effects of changing coaches because the running game is the simplest facet of any offense and will be the primary method of advancing the ball if possible and feasible. In many cases, a change in coaching staff can actually help a running back post bigger numbers, because as a new offense is being installed, the running game may be the only part that works well initially. One major caveat here—make sure the running back reasonably fits into the plans of the new regime. After all, he's no longer the head coach's "guy" and could be subjected to a change in the backfield.

2. **Offensive Line**   This is both a critical and yet difficult-to-assess area. Unlike the quarterback, who merely needs the linemen to get in the way of the rush on a pass play long enough for him to throw the ball, the running back needs those linemen for much more. There are guards who may need to pull to the other side, tackles that must direct the defensive end away from the play, and a center who has to snap the ball and immediately take on a nose guard. All these players work in unison to create a particular hole for the runner and yet no openings for the linebackers. The longer a unit works together, the better they are. Look

for how mature the line is and particularly if it contains any Pro Bowl (or should have been Pro Bowl) players.

3. **Health Issues** A true full-time-duty running back will likely get blasted 20 times or more every game. It is the nature of the position when the player takes a handoff in the middle of the field and must get past at least the front line of the defense. In most seasons, only about half of NFL teams manage to have full-time backs play for at least 15 games in a season. Durability is a major issue with running backs, and it is more than a coincidence that the best backs have lost very little time while recuperating. Medical science has progressed to a point where a knee injury that would end a career a mere decade ago now heals within a year or two. Never overvalue a back still in the process of recovery. By the same token, unless there is a track record of injury, do not overestimate the chance a back will be injured. They all will be and it is merely a question of when and how often.

4. **Passing Game** The effectiveness of a passing game plays directly into the success of the rushing game and vice versa. Ideally, a team wants enough balance so that opponents cannot load up against either the run or pass, which begets only more success from less focus on any one aspect. Consider how well the team will be passing for the upcoming season and that will play into what to expect from the running game. Obviously the running back should be factored into the passing game and typically will have bigger years receiving when the passing game is not working well enough to make enough use of wideouts much farther down the field. All aspects of the offense are interrelated, even if rushing generally comes first in the game plan.

5. **Specialists** The best-case scenario is that a running back plays a role that includes "never coming off the field." That is becoming less common. The use of third-down backs and short-yardage bulls cuts into the production of a tailback even if it does save his wear and tear. The NFL team wants that running back fresh all the way to the Super Bowl. You want him to be run ragged until his tongue hangs out every week. The age and health of a back can indicate whether a specialist role may be created this year, as will a change in coaching staff.

6. **Defense** One overlooked area is the overall expectations of the defense and the effect on the rushing game. The better the defense, the better the running game because of improved field position. A defense is a running back's best friend when it can keep the opponent behind on the scoreboard and thereby increase the offense's need to just control the ball and clock for the rest of the game. A bad defense means a team will be falling behind more often, which only kicks in the need to throw the ball more often. It is no surprise that teams that have the best defenses usually have one of the better running games as well.

7. **Schedule** The running back is the only offensive ball-handler who will consistently be given 20 to 30 opportunities each game to gain yardage. Even the best wide receiver usually has no more than seven to 10 plays go to him per week and he catches far fewer. The more a player is used, the more that opposing defense is either allowing or preventing him from having a good game. There is no position as sensitive to the schedule as running back, and at least a cursory view of the up-

coming schedule should be considered in valuing that position. Ideally, you should have expectations of what will happen for the entire season including those critical fantasy playoff weeks. TheHuddle.com and many other magazines and Web sites evaluate the upcoming schedule for every team.

Running backs are the closest to "plug and play" players as there are on an offense and yet that does not separate them from the dynamics of the team around them. Coaching changes have less bearing on how well a back does and can even help him, but the effectiveness of the rushing game and the defense will either limit or increase what the runner can accomplish. Unless a team has the luxury of running the ball on most plays, even the most talented back will be rendered average.

STUD REPEATABILITY

Studs are always beneficial for fantasy positions like running back and wide receiver, and typically there will be two or three players from those positions started weekly. This means while owning a stud running back is a big advantage, your team will need at least two serviceable backs to compete each week. First off, let's take a 10-year look at the top five fantasy backs to see where they ended up the following season (see figure 7.1).

Since 2000, top five running backs have fared well in repeating good performances. But it is troublesome that in most years at least one back tumbles below the level of a fantasy starter (most often that happens due to injury). Such was the case in 1999 when Jamal Anderson, Terrell Davis, Fred Taylor, and Garrison Hearst all lost

WHERE TOP 5 RUNNING BACKS FINISHED THEIR NEXT SEASON				
Ended	Top 5	6th–10th	11th–20th	>20th
1997	1	1	2	1
1998	1	1	1	2
1999	1	0	0	4
2000	3	0	2	0
2001	2	0	1	2
2002	2	0	3	0
2003	3	2	0	0
2004	1	0	3	1
2005	3	0	1	1
2006	2	1	1	1

Figure 7.1

time to injury, if not the entire season. Again in 2004, Jamal Lewis, Priest Holmes, and Ahman Green lost time due to injury as well.

What the ten-year chart shows is that while running backs prior to 2000 were having a hard time holding on to top five production the following season, since that time there has been remarkable "repeatability" that is usually denied only because of injury. No wonder running backs fly off the shelves from the start—they deserve that priority from their contribution and consistency for the big-name players.

Beware though, the magic year phenomenon that has a player suddenly produce far better than they normally would due to a beneficial combination of team dynamics and their schedule. In past years players like Curtis Martin, Jamal Lewis, Mike Anderson,

Stephen Davis, and Fred Taylor have turned in monster seasons only to fade the next year. Actually they were not fading; they were merely returning to the level of production that they are typically capable of turning in each year. The big-game guys, those with great opportunity, situation, and talent, are most likely to repeat.

Those next-tier backs who should round out the best #1 starting running backs in your league are not nearly as consistent as those top backs. Up through 2000, drafting a tailback who ended second-tier (sixth to 10th best) during the previous season meant getting what you paid for or better in most cases. But over the next six years those numbers tailed off and usually only one player actually improved, just one remained the same, and three others fell back to being more of a #2 starting running back, if that (see figure 7.2). Important to remember

WHERE 6TH TO 10TH BEST RUNNING BACKS FINISHED THEIR NEXT SEASON

Ended	Top 5	6th–10th	11th–20th	>20th
1997	2	2	1	0
1998	2	1	2	0
1999	1	2	0	2
2000	0	3	0	2
2001	1	0	0	4
2002	2	0	2	1
2003	0	1	3	1
2004	1	1	2	1
2005	1	1	3	0
2006	1	0	0	4

Figure 7.2

though—you will likely need at least two starting tailbacks and even a drop from sixth best to 20th best is not a team-killer. Considering that, drafting running backs early from this tier still produced a starter about four out of five times. Maybe not quite as good as you bragged on draft day, but it's still respectable and worthy of a high draft pick. Again—this is why the first round in fantasy drafts loves running backs. They are the highest-scoring, most consistent, and the lowest risk to select. Oh yes, and you need two or more of them.

The top 20 backs are all fantasy-relevant and deserve scrutiny, but with only 32 teams in the NFL currently, even below-average rushers are still needed as fantasy starters in most leagues. Each season typically has about 24 or more teams with rock-solid (or at least reliable) situations as to which runner will be getting the most opportunity for that team. Those teams that do not have a clear-cut primary back can produce runners with very nice fantasy numbers for the season, but it is much less common. Always take the safer picks on running backs, the ones who will reasonably have the best opportunities to rack up yardage and scores. No fantasy fanatic can resist targeting a couple of runners who they believe will have a dramatic increase in production—but never overpay for them. History shows that the risk is not worth the reward.

WHERE SLEEPERS COME FROM

If you could grant one wish to fantasy veterans, it would likely be knowledge of who the sleeper running backs were going to be the next season. Hitting a sleeper back can be very tough because literally every league mate is looking for the very same thing and there's plenty of information out there to spark interest in almost any player. But the best of all worlds is finding that back who not only exceeds expectations but also ends up as a top five back that year. Consider the same ten-year stretch for where top five running backs came from the previous season (see figure 7.3).

WHERE RUNNING BACKS FINISHED THE PREVIOUS SEASON BEFORE A TOP 5 YEAR

Ended	Top 5	6th–10th	11th–20th	>20th
1997	1	2	1	1
1998	1	2	1	1
1999	1	1	1	2
2000	3	0	0	2
2001	2	1	0	2
2002	2	2	0	1
2003	3	0	2	0
2004	1	1	3	0
2005	3	1	0	1
2006	2	0	2	1

Figure 7.3

As we have seen before, prior to the 2000 season there was amazing consistency year to year, while there was more variation in recent times. Other than 2000 and 2004, most of the top five came from the top 10 of the previous season. Sadly only a couple of running backs since 2001 were true sleepers who rose from at a sub-20th-best performance the previous year (if they even played at all). The last few seasons have seen aging veterans turning in good years despite being older than what once was considered over the hill.

Considering a sample of running backs who went from ending a season ranked less than 20th to leaping up to a top five finish the following year (see Appendix, Table III), four were rookies. In fact each of these players was in their first year as a true starter. Ahman Green and Priest Holmes came from other teams who would not use them and were finally given the opportunity that they needed to shine. Napoleon Kaufman, Stephen Davis, Mike Anderson, and Larry Johnson all had big years when they were given the starting nod once the primary back from the previous year left for another team or was injured. You want a true sleeper type? Take a player in his first season as a starter with opportunity to play as a full-time player for the first time in the NFL. While not every first-year starter is top five, every top five sleeper has been a first-year starter.

Running backs are needed in more depth than quarterbacks, so a further review of the position is warranted. Figure 7.4 is a breakdown of what those running backs who ended sixth to 10th in one season did the previous season.

WHERE RUNNING BACKS FINISHED THE SEASON BEFORE THEIR 6TH TO 10TH RANKING

Ended	Top 5	6th–10th	11th–20th	>20th
1997	1	2	1	1
1998	1	1	2	1
1999	0	2	1	2
2000	0	3	1	1
2001	0	0	3	2
2002	0	0	3	2
2003	2	1	2	0
2004	0	1	1	3
2005	0	1	2	2
2006	1	1	1	2

Figure 7.4

Through 2000, the carryover year to year was much higher. Since that time usually a sixth to 10th best running back experienced a decline the next year in about four out of five occasions on average. The biggest concern here is that about two out of five usually fell below the level of what would be a decent starting tailback, which once again indicates why taking safer picks at running back is a good idea in the first round.

Sleepers typically come from a player in his first season either as a rookie, as a backup who became a starter, or a stud player who had been out injured for a year (see Appendix, Table IV). Think about your recent past with fantasy football. How many times did a player who had been "promising" for a year or two become the sleeper darling in drafts only to prove that his potential once again exceeded his production?

For backups stepping up, there is really no one indicator that says it will happen, because that entails forecasting when the primary back will go down injured. Every fantasy draft in the world entails everyone stealing the backup running backs for other fantasy teams and yet so few of those actually pan out. Ideally, back up your own running backs and you are better off in a majority of cases—as hard as that can be.

BREAKOUT YEARS

Sleepers are often players who are having a breakout season and are undervalued because they have never produced big numbers previously. The hunt for running backs with potential is red-hot in virtually every league, so taking cues from the past can help give you an edge over those fellow league mates who fall into conventional thinking that has been more than a little impacted by sheer hype.

The majority of breakouts occur in the player's first full season with a team and almost always it will be the team that originally drafted them (see Appendix, Table V). The years that the player has been in the NFL do not matter much, only that he has a great opportunity for the first time in his career. It is also notable that those running backs who broke out in their first full season are also the same list of running backs who were top fantasy backs for most of their career.

ROOKIES

While there is almost no reason to draft a rookie quarterback, the same is not true for first-year running backs. They have definite value but that is very easy to overestimate. For those of you who have been playing fantasy football for more than 10 years, you can blame the 1995 draft for propping up the fantasy hopes for running backs drafted deeper in the NFL draft. Consider that after Ki-Jana Carter, Tyrone Wheatley, Napoleon Kaufman, and six other running backs were selected that year, the third round offered up Curtis Martin to the Patriots, sandwiched between William Henderson and Zack Crockett, who technically were actually fullbacks. Then, after Dino Philyaw was snatched up by the Patriots with the 195th overall pick during the sixth round, the Broncos took a chance on Terrell Davis with the next pick. Yes, the Patriots could have ended up with both Martin and Davis from the same draft using third- and sixth-round picks. Though the Davis pick is more than a decade past, there are still fantasy fans searching deeper in drafts for similar gems. Forget about it.

Terrell Davis was obscured in the draft because at Georgia he was Garrison Hearst's backup after transferring from Long Beach State. Never base drafting decisions on the exception to rules, let alone extreme exceptions to rules. Over a six-year period, there has been no running back drafted deeper than the fourth round who has managed any significant value at any time in their career, let alone their rookie season. None.

What rookie backs need—and both Curtis Martin and Terrell Davis received—was the opportunity to become the full-time starter to begin the season. For a back drafted that deeply to get that chance is obviously rare and not getting any more common.

From 2000 to 2005, LaDainian Tomlinson was the only rookie running back who produced well enough to be a fantasy team's best running back (see Appendix, Table VI). Considering a league of 12 teams, the only rookies who managed to make it in the top 24 during their rookie season (and therefore being worthy of being a starter in leagues with two starting running backs per team) were Tomlinson, Jamal Lewis, Carnell Williams, Kevin Jones, and Ronnie Brown. That was just five players over a six-year period that included 2005, which had been heralded as the "most running back rich" draft in perhaps two decades or more. Two thousand six proved the best rookie class with Maurice Jones Drew ending up as a top 10; and Reggie Bush used a late season push to reach the top 20, as did Joseph Addai. It was a freak year.

The beauty and allure of a rookie running back is that he can deliver decent numbers from the start—it does happen. However, considering the number of first-round running backs who never delivered their first year shows the great risk against minimal reward for drafting one too early. Face it, these are the players who have no NFL track record so their best quality is that they played very well in college and have yet to prove they are not merely an average NFL player or worse. During the 1990s and earlier, there were more rookie running backs who showed up big their first season; however, in the complicated offenses and trends that exist in the NFL currently, those first-year runners are just not receiving the opportunity as they once would have. Consider the number of those running backs who went to a team that already had a proven runner. Then remember that none of them ended up with significant fantasy value in their first season while sharing or even just watching the primary back continue to play.

In fantasy football, rookie tailbacks are judged far less on talent than they are on their situation—they need that full-time opportunity to generate fantasy points. Taking one too early in the hope that his team's starting tailback will go down and allow him to become a star (like Mike Anderson) is rare enough that it is not worth giving much weight. It just never happens . . . well, almost never.

Rookie running backs are often very exciting and hit the ground running (literally) only to find that a 16-game season is a bit longer than the dozen or so games he was used to in college. First-year players are often injured at least a bit in their first season, if only with hamstring issues from legs not used to this level of effort. Unless the situation and opportunity appear superior, in most cases you are better off shying away from rookie running backs. After all, even if you are certain of his opportunity and situation, his talent level is still just an educated guess, unlike all the other veterans with a track record to consider. Figure that NFL scouts' sole purpose is to find talent and even they get it horribly wrong sometimes. Do you really know more than a scout who has spent the last 20 years personally viewing live performances and workouts to determine the talent level of rookies?

In the perfect draft, your starting running backs would be veterans who offer the optimal mixture of risk and reward. Only in later rounds should you blend in first-year players as backups. There are plenty of chances later on to take risks in fantasy drafts—why take one early on a player with the least known about him in the most productive and consistent position?

DRAFT PLANS

Using the step approach—creating projections initially based on previous season statistics and then modifying them based on the seven concerns listed earlier in the chapter—is a sound approach to coming up with solid rankings for running backs.

Beware of all the preseason hype and conventional wisdom that is easy to obtain in magazines and on the Internet and make your rankings on your own. Preparing for your draft will include selecting at least one and maybe even two running backs in the first two rounds. While there are instances where you can start your draft with top wideouts or quarterbacks and forgo running backs until the third round, that strategy will usually result in a season-long uphill battle in which you struggle to find suitable players for what should be your most consistent point producers. Using a LAG will indicate how running backs stack up against the other fantasy positions, but reality says that pretty much every league out there will covet running backs. And ask yourself this question—is it easier to make up ground on a quarterback, running back, tight end, or wide receiver?

The initial rounds of a draft are no place to be taking unnecessary risks, and invariably more risk exists for positions other than running back. This is not to say that grabbing a top quarterback, wideout, or even tight end can make sense in the first two rounds of a draft (depending largely on what your LAG indicates for comparative value), but wait until later rounds to act on hunches and you'll be right far more than you will be wrong. Drafting players should always be predicated on risk and reward, and that means you have to get those running backs ranked correctly—there just is no waiting on the best ones.

BACKUP RUNNING
BACKS

8

Captain Knauer: Dammit, Warden, I think this game's a big mistake.

Warden Hazen: Captain, not only will you have the chance to hone our team to a fine edge, you'll also have the opportunity to learn a great deal about life. Why is it, do you suppose, that I can walk through this yard, surrounded by hate, and in total command?

Captain Knauer: Because you've got 15 gun turrets all around you that say you can.

(From The Longest Yard, *1974)*

INJURY IS A REALITY in the NFL and there is no position where that is more apparent than running back. They do not have 15 gun turrets covering them but they do have 11 defenders more than willing to knock them out of a game. While quarterbacks get blasted and receivers go across the middle and get creamed, the running back crashes into defenders usually 20 to 30 times each game. And as we all know, running backs are the biggest problem for fantasy teams.

The reasoning is simple enough. In most leagues there will be only one quarterback started each week and there are often a few actual starting quarterbacks still on the waiver wire. This would never happen with running backs. There are only a dozen or so tight ends worth owning, so while there is always depth on them, no one really cares. And wideouts? Including the slot position, there are a whopping 96 starters every week in the NFL. Unless you are playing in a 10-man league, starting backs are going to be scarce.

Given these realities, running backs are the only fantasy position that actually calls for drafting a backup player. Quarterbacks get hurt less often and there are often better players on the waiver wire than their backup would be. There is no such thing as a backup wideout per se, just a depth chart with more receivers to call up. But running backs offer a clear line of succession on the depth chart, and chances are that their backups will be drafted—either to insure a starter or as a gamble that bad things happen to a primary back that someone else owns. When non–running backs are injured, everyone in the league snickers and then checks the league rosters to see who just lost a player. When a running back is hurt, everyone in the league immediately checks to see if his backup is still available. And then they snicker at the other team's misfortune.

Over the five-year sample period (see figure 8.1), on average half of the first 20 running backs drafted were unable to play a full 16-game season, and this does not even include the eight other running backs who missed only one game. While 2001 was an extreme year that witnessed a dozen running backs miss a combined total of 103 games, the next year was relatively light, with just eight players missing a shockingly low 19 games. The next three years are more indicative of what to expect—roughly half of those running backs who are drafted to be starters in your league are going to miss at least two games and could miss the entire season—as I so painfully discovered in 2001 (thanks for nothing, Jamal). There will usually be about 50 games during the season that a backup will be starting instead of the normal starter.

Before we consider backup running backs, it is important to make a distinction between the types of running backs that are currently in the NFL and therefore on fantasy teams. There are seven different categories of running back to consider.

TOP 20 RB'S DRAFTED 2002–2006: WHEN DRAFTED VS. NUMBER OF GAMES MISSED

#	2002	Gms	#	2003	Gms	#	2004	Gms
1	M Faulk	2	2	M Faulk	5	1	P Holmes	8
3	A Green	2	3	C Portis	2	5	D McAllister	3
5	P Holmes	2	8	T Henry	2	8	J Lewis	5
8	A Thomas	4	9	E James	3	10	F Taylor	2
10	E James	2	14	S Davis	2	14	T Henry	12
11	S Davis	2	15	C Garner	5	15	M Bennett	10
13	D McAllister	1	16	C Dillon	4	16	S Davis	14
15	J Bettis	4	17	W Green	10	17	C Brown	4
			20	J Stewart	16	18	M Faulk	2
						19	K Jones	2
						20	T Jones	3

#	2005	Gms	#	2006	Gms
3	P Holmes	8	1	S Alexander	6
4	D McAllister	11	8	R Brown	3
6	D Davis	4	9	C Williams	2
7	K Jones	3	10	L Jordan	7
10	J Jones	3	11	C Portis	8
11	C Dillon	3	12	W McGahee	2
16	C Martin	3	13	B Westbrook	1
17	A Green	11	18	K Jones	4
18	C Williams	2	20	R Droughns	2
19	B Westbrook	3			

Figure 8.1

1. **The Super Back** The do-everything, "don't come off the field" studs who everyone loves in fantasy football. They run, they catch, and they don't much share the ball either. Past examples—LaDainian Tomlinson, Shaun Alexander, Edgerrin James, Larry Johnson. (Just look at the top of your RB rankings.)

2. **The Run Back** Some teams employ a two-back system where one player will perform the primary rushing while another is more of a receiving back. Little role in the passing game but all things rushing are his. Past examples—Corey Dillon, Rudi Johnson.

3. **The Catch Back** Plays for a team that loves to throw to a running back so much that in many games he will actually have more yardage receiving than he will rushing. Past examples—Brian Westbrook, LaMont Jordan.

4. **The Split Back** Works in a system that truly uses two backs with both filling the same role as the other player. A fantasy nightmare usually, at least in knowing what could have been. These situations rarely last more than a season or two before one takes over or the other one leaves. Past examples—Thomas Jones/ Cedric Benson, Frank Gore/Kevan Barlow.

5. **The Third-Down Back** Works mostly on third-down passing situations but in enough volume that he has fantasy value, at least in reception point leagues. Examples—Kevin Faulk, Tony Fisher, Chris Perry.

6. **The Yardage Back** A tailback who operates in a two-back system but who will generally run and catch and won't be as big a factor in short yardage or near the goal

line. Typically these players are fast, have high yards per carry, and don't normally score many touchdowns. Past examples—Warrick Dunn, Willie Parker, Tatum Bell.

7. **The Goal Line Back** The other half of a yardage back, the player who usually only carries when it is tough yards for a first down or near the goal line where his bulk and ability to be a bull scores touchdowns. Past examples—Jerome Bettis, Brandon Jacobs, T. J. Duckett.

It is worth noting that while some running backs are locked into their role for their entire career, others will transition to a new category from season to season and even from game to game depending on the team's needs and situation. The roles also can reflect where players are in their career. Many start out with more limited duty as a goal line back or a catch back until the aging primary rusher finally leaves or actually switches positions with him (case in point—Steven Jackson and Marshall Faulk). Older backs often play out their career as catch backs if they still have speed and little bulk or they decline to a TD-scoring role, as we saw with the classic example of Jerome Bettis. Fantasy nirvana is a super back playing between the ages of 23 and 30.

Not all running backs are equal. I would strongly argue that it is the most interchangeable position in fantasy football. I'd argue it both strongly and at length if you are buying the beer. But it is important to note the different categories of running backs because grabbing backups for players makes more or less sense depending on what category back they currently are—and, most importantly, what sort of back they would be if given the opportunity to replace the primary back. For some keys, let's consider the best and worst replacement running backs over a five-year sample period (see figure 8.2).

10 BEST REPLACEMENT RUNNING BACK PERFORMANCES 2001–2005

Year	Starter	Backup	Gms	Rush Yds	Rcv Yds	TD's	FF Pts	Avg. Pts
2005	Priest Holmes	Larry Johnson	8	1,150	255	14	224.5	28
2004	Priest Holmes	Larry Johnson	6	541	248	11	144.9	24
2001	Ricky Watters	Shaun Alexander	14	1,318	343	16	262.1	19
2004	Stephen Davis	Nick Goings	8	712	284	7	141.6	18
2001	Marshall Faulk	Trung Canidate	2	195	37	2	35.2	18
2002	Edgerrin James	James Mungro	2	174	53	2	34.7	17
2004	Travis Henry	Willis McGahee	12	1,097	157	13	203.4	17
2001	Edgerrin James	Dominic Rhodes	10	961	216	8	165.7	17
2005	Domanick Davis	Jonathan Wells	4	287	106	4	63.3	16
2005	Ahman Green	Samkon Gado	7	582	77	7	107.9	15

Figure 8.2

The types of backups that had the best showing were naturally ones that played on teams that had the better offenses at the time, notably Kansas City, Seattle, St. Louis, and Indianapolis. While perhaps not exactly plug-in-and-get-the-same-performance, the backups on those high-powered offenses consistently fared very well when they had their opportunity. It helped the Seahawks to be sitting on the top draft pick of Alexander at the time, but recall that prior to Ricky Watters being injured Alexander had been in the NFL for 19 games and only produced a total of 340 rushing yards.

Those super backs like Priest Holmes, Ricky Watters, Marshall Faulk, and Edgerrin James were almost exclusively used prior to injury and their replacements marched in with great performances. Alexander and Larry Johnson continued to be great backs but Nick Goings, Trung Canidate, James Mungro, and Dominic Rhodes never became hot free agents for a reason. They played in a great offense and were able to get the opportunity to shine. But in a league with so many talented backs there was no demand to turn them into starters elsewhere.

Notable also were Nick Goings and Samkon Gado, who did not play for teams with monster offenses at the time; but the dynamics were such that literally all other tailbacks were injured at the time and they received a rather heavy load when they played. Both had fine contributions because they had opportunity and situation working in their favor. This is not really any different from what the wideout Muhsin Muhammad managed in 2004 when he realistically became almost the only target for Jake Delhomme that year and ended up leading the league. It is opportunity that matters most with a running back. Even Jonathan Wells managed to sneak in with a top 10 backup performance thanks to a Houston offense that did not share the ball elsewhere.

Lastly and perhaps most importantly, consider the value of owning a backup who was picked early in the NFL draft. Shaun Alexander, Larry Johnson, and Willis McGahee were all first-round picks by their respective franchises and were billed as the "future" of their teams. All three stepped in after the starter went down with injury. Teams do not spend #1 picks on a back just to have a flashy backup. They acquire them to take the reins whenever the current starter no longer can carry the load.

So the best backups to grab are always the players who are waiting for a super back to be injured. If you own a top 10 back—and

10 WORST REPLACEMENT RUNNING BACK PERFORMANCES 2001–2005

Year	Starter	Backup	Gms	Rush Yds	Rcv Yds	TD's	FF Pts	Avg. Pts
2001	James Stewart	Lamont Warren	6	128	181	3	48.9	8
2005	Deuce McAllister	Antowain Smith	10	531	39	3	75	8
2005	Curtis Martin	Cedric Houston	3	172	42	0	21.4	7
2003	James Stewart	Shawn Bryson	16	606	340	3	112.6	7
2001	Michael Bennett	Doug Chapman	3	117	64	0	18.1	6
2001	Fred Taylor	Elvis Joseph	12	294	183	2	59.7	5
2002	Anthony Thomas	Adrian Peterson	4	101	18	1	17.9	4
2003	Travis Henry	Joe Burns	2	39	40	0	7.9	4
2004	Fred Taylor	Greg Jones	2	68	1	0	6.9	3
2004	Chris Brown	Robert Holcombe	4	30	52	0	8.2	2

Figure 8.3

likely you will have at least one—determine when you need to get their backup (roster-space-dependent). You know when your star running back is suddenly injured that his backup will be taken with the first free agent pick of the week. The team matters to a running back and their scheme and blocking ability will translate into nice fantasy points regardless if it is Larry Johnson or Shaun Alexander, or just Nick Goings, James Mungro, or Dominic Rhodes.

Now let's look at the worst backup performances in recent years (see figure 8.3).

Notice the difference in how these backs were used in the passing game—not much. While the top 10 backups almost all averaged between 20 and 40 yards per game receiving, the worst backups had only three over 14 yards per game, and only one had more than 21 yards per game receiving. None of these backs was used fully and you have to admit—this is a pretty motley crew. However—would Rhodes, Mungro, Goings, etc., have done any better given those teams and their situations? Probably not.

Also, notice how many of the injured starters were *not* super backs in the first place. They weren't split backs either—these players were rarely used prior to the primary back's injury. A nice example is Fred Taylor, who seemingly always demanded his fantasy owner to carry a backup, but in reality the bang for the buck was not that great. It is a good indicator that Taylor was playing far above what the offense would normally allow and that his previous success was as much about him as it was about his scheme and team. It only takes a glance to see that other than Taylor none of the worst backups played for a team with an average rushing game (if even in the top 25).

Hence, our next rule:

Rule 9

The better your running back, the more important that you own his backup.

While this may seem obvious to some, check your league to see how many of those teams with the best backs actually own their respective backup. Most team owners will wait until after they have acquired almost all of their required starters (other than defenses and kickers) before they worry about getting the backup. That means beyond around the eighth round in most leagues. And the longer they wait, the greater the chance that their backup will be snaked by another team looking for some midseason coup or at least some trade bait to dangle in front of you.

Think of it this way—those best backs that you burn a first-round pick on will be your most consistent if not highest-scoring player. And they will also likely be the ones that have backups who will shine if given the opportunity that comes, on average, for about half of the backs drafted for at least two games or more.

You need to weigh what other players are available, obviously, and if it appears you can make a stronger play for another while losing your #1 RB backup, then so be it. But over time you'll see most of those deeper speculation picks on running backs won't pan out while you are scanning the waiver wire for a third-down back because your stud just wrenched his knee and the waiver wire is rather sparse in that position.

By no means should you back up all your running backs, even if you have the chance and roster room. Recognize and apply the different categories of running back before backing up. If a running back becomes a starter in your league—grab him because you just never know. But always try to insure that first-round pick with his backup. You'll reap the dividends if the unthinkable becomes the unavoidable. Even if it means skipping on that fourth wideout who will likely never mean much anyway.

WIDE RECEIVERS

Rod Tidwell: I am a valuable commodity! I go across the middle! I see a dude coming at me, trying to kill me, I tell myself "Get killed. Catch the ball!" BOO YA! Touchdown! I make miracles happen!

Jerry Maguire: How's your head?

Rod Tidwell: Bubblicious.

(From Jerry Maguire, 1996)

UNDERSTANDING WIDE RECEIVERS is one of the most critical and yet most challenging tasks in fantasy football. Unlike running backs and quarterbacks, a wideout has a complicated role on an offensive play. He must get off the line cleanly and into his exact route so that the quarterback knows where to look for him. He has to get enough separation from the defensive backs so that the quarterback considers him as the best option. He must then catch the ball, often at top speed, and that pass may be coming over his shoulder, drilled as a fastball into his chest, or lofted a mighty jump and fingertip catch away. Oh yes, and he must actually catch and hold on to the ball while every defensive back turns his attention to crushing him without the nuisance of wading through any blockers.

Great receivers are not born overnight and they are not created on a practice field. When reviewing wideouts, realize that the equation for success of the wide receiver is different from those for quarterbacks and running backs:

Rule 10

WR Value = (Talent × 2) × Situation × Opportunity

As always, talent is expression of natural ability, attitude, preparation, and hard work. And for a position that takes longer to learn and master, a wide receiver must exemplify those attributes to have significant fantasy value because he is merely the conclusion of a passing play that could have any number of endings, and only one involves him catching the ball and gaining yards.

It is more than mere opportunity—there are always multiple receivers on any given play. Situation matters, but most teams average between 30 and 35 passes per game. Just being on the field is not enough with so many options for the quarterback; it is all about talent, which makes a wideout become a preferred target with consistency and productivity. Consider too that success only breeds more coverage by the defense, so the best of the best are more than just incrementally better than the other receivers on their teams.

One last qualifier for wide receiver success is not quantifiable. He needs to be crazy. Maybe not so much the "wear a foil hat to prevent alien abduction" sort of crazy. He needs to be a bit off-center in that obsessively dedicated, fearless, and often more than a little conceited type of way. A receiver has no blockers. He is going over the middle at times to catch passes in the heart of the defense. There is perhaps no job on the team that demands as much courage as the wide receiver and he needs to be completely confident in his abilities. He needs to be "crazy good." Many come across as egotistical and self-centered but that is merely a by-product of their need for supreme confidence. After all, he needs to feel "bubblicious" on every play.

CONCERNS AND ADJUSTMENTS

Thanks to their sheer number and varying role in every game, no other position enjoys as many breakout seasons as does wide receiver. After reviewing past statistics both overall and per game to create your initial projections, there are several concerns that you must apply to those calculated numbers before you can be confident you have nailed down the toughest position to project:

1. **Coaching Changes** The worst impact to a wideout is a change in offensive scheme typically brought about by a coaching change. As noted, a pass play is fairly complex in terms of what has to happen, and that means all players on the offense have to be well versed in their roles for the wide receiver to even get a pass thrown to him. Despite the reality that most teams suffer through a losing record when they swap out coaching staff, the fact that the team will be behind in the score often does not necessarily equate to meaning that the wideout is going to get a ton more catches. He may well have a higher number of passing targets, but can actually decrease in production from the previous season. Even top wide receivers in the league will suffer at least a bit with a change in scheme and coaches, at least for the first half of the season while the offense begins to form chemistry and execute the plays as they were designed. In fantasy football, a slow start can be death for your season.

2. **Passing Game** You must determine what role the wideout is expected to play in the offense. If the same scheme is being used and the same players—includ-

ing quarterback—are still on the team from the prior season, will there be any reason to expect a change in the roles of the wideouts? Is the receiver you are reviewing the clear #1 target or is there reason to believe that the #2 wideout is about to break out and supplant him as the primary receiver? Is there any reason to expect either tight ends or running backs to increase or decrease their role in the passing game? By the same token, is the scheme just now taking effect after a year or so after being installed?

3. **Health Issues**   Fortunately, wide receivers generally are among the healthiest players and every season typically has at least 50 to 60 wide receivers who play in 15 or 16 games. Wide receivers are also most often of two types—players that never get injured and players that rarely stay healthy. While age has a significant effect on NFL players, it affects wide receivers far less than most. Don't be concerned that a wideout is over 30 years of age. The top 20 wideouts in any given season will contain five to 10 players over 30 years old. This position requires a lengthy learning curve and the best wideouts are very experienced. Unless there is a demonstrable reason to assume otherwise, consider an older player to be more valuable than a younger one. The only true injury of major concern with wideouts are ligament tears in the knees, which rob the player of burst, speed, and the ability to cut sharply, but medical science now can do wonders for a player committed to rehabilitation. Do not overvalue past health issues with a wide receiver unless he has proven to be injury-prone. However—the safest play is to not draft a wideout coming off a major knee injury. A few turn in decent seasons, most fall far short, and almost none meet the expectations of the drafter.

4. **Rushing Game** The better the rushing game, the worse the passing game will be. Rushing the ball is a far safer action than passing and is preferred by NFL offenses, all things being equal. From 2001 to 2005, the 25 times that teams were in the top five for rushing yards in a season, only six of them were in the top 10 for passing yards. Of the 15 top three rushing teams in that time period, none did better than 12th overall in passing yards. The top rushing team was never better than 22nd in passing and four of those were 27th or worse. It is an obvious inverse relationship between rushing and receiving that should be considered when determining what expectations to have of a wide receiver.

5. **Is He the #1 WR?** While a few offenses will have two wideouts with significant fantasy value, the average team has one true primary wideout and one secondary target. The preferred wideout can be either the split end or the flanker, depending on the team, but only the #1 wideout produces significant fantasy points and any amount of consistency for most NFL teams. The better his team's running game is, the less you should expect from the passing game overall, though #1 wideouts tend to maintain their role while secondary receivers end up with declining numbers. In individual games with big passing numbers, both starting wide receivers will usually share in the bounty.

6. **Learning Curve** The third-year phenomenon was traditionally a near guaranteed role where the receiver would do almost nothing in his first season, then show signs of improvement in his second season before exploding on the scene in his third season. That is not nearly as true anymore. NFL teams are less interested in

developing players now that the salary cap constraints and free agency mean that players are only locked to a team for about their first three or four years. NFL teams now throw their top rookie talent into the line-ups more as a rule than an exception. What we have seen since 2000 are receivers in their second or even rookie seasons having significant fantasy value. That all draws back to the initial argument—talent is king with fantasy wide receivers and that either shows up early or not at all in most cases. Look for an upward progression of production from a wide receiver that can suggest continued improvement—but once again, his opportunity, situation, and especially talent are going to be key to his fantasy value.

7. **Defense** Just as the rushing game suppresses the passing, the better the defense is, the less a team will find itself in a shootout that entails plenty of balls thrown. Consider those top defenses from the previous season—did they have great passing games or were they primarily run first and pass last? The better the defense is at holding down the score, the less a team will need to pass the ball. Ball control is a goal of every offense, and with a lead to protect and a clock to drain, passing the ball just does not make sense on most plays. One caveat here: The #1 wideout can maintain his production levels because he will always be the primary receiver. Great defenses typically affect the secondary receivers much more since there is less need to get them involved in the game.

8. **Schedule** While the schedule has a major impact on running backs and quarterbacks, it is less so for the individual receivers. A tougher schedule can benefit wideouts because the team may need to pass more—

WHERE TOP 5 WIDE RECEIVERS FINISHED THEIR NEXT SEASON

Ended	Top 5	6th–10th	11th–20th	>20th
1997	0	2	0	3
1998	1	1	1	2
1999	1	0	0	4
2000	2	1	1	1
2001	4	0	0	1
2002	2	0	0	2
2003	1	1	1	1
2004	0	2	1	1
2005	0	1	0	4
2006	1	1	1	2

Figure 9.1

but facing superior defenses doesn't help. Unless a team will have a brutal passing schedule the next year, don't concern yourself with it.

STUD REPEATABILITY

There is nothing like ending up with a stud receiver who will score as well as most any running back. Each season witnesses a few top wideouts repeating a great year, and there are always a few players who turn in career-best seasons that give them a pass to the top of most draft boards the next season. But how predictive is a great season for a wideout?

Figure 9.1 shows a dose of reality about top five wideouts. If you remove the "uber-studs," Marvin Harrison (7), Randy Moss (6), Terrell Owens (4), Chad Johnson (3), and Rod Smith (3), no other wideout appeared in the top five more than twice in the ten-year sample. Only four players qualified with double showings—Cris Carter, Antonio Freeman, and Eric Moulds. That makes eight players who had repeated top five years at least once in the sample while 22 other players only came up truly big just one time. Other than a player who has repeatedly been in the top five, it is nearly a lock that a top five wideout will NOT repeat the following year.

Since there are so many wideouts needed in a fantasy league, consider what the next level of wideout did the following season once they had ended a season ranked sixth through 10th:

WHERE 6TH TO 10TH BEST WIDE RECEIVERS FINISHED THEIR NEXT SEASON

Ended	Top 5	6th–10th	11th–20th	>20th
1997	1	1	2	1
1998	0	1	1	3
1999	2	0	1	2
2000	0	1	1	3
2001	0	2	1	2
2002	0	1	2	2
2003	0	0	3	2
2004	0	0	2	3
2005	1	1	1	2
2006	1	1	1	2

Figure 9.2

Other than a freak season in 1999, most years only witness one player rise to the top level the next season and normally none of them do so. What's just as bad is that in most seasons, three or four will actually go down in production the next season. One major reason is that a wideout experiences a magic year where his situation and opportunity suddenly come together to create great production and then he returns to his normal level of production the following season. This most often happens when the other starting wideout for the team is injured or the team has major problems that lead to them being woefully behind in most games and forced to throw far more than desired.

WHERE SLEEPERS COME FROM

While most fantasy players will rely heavily on those prior-year statistics, what is the reality about where those elite top five wideouts came from the prior year? They usually do not come from the previous top five receivers.

Almost like a bell curve, wideouts peaked in 2001 and 2002 with an uncharacteristically high number of top five players repeating, but in most seasons the majority of top five wideouts came from either the 11th to 20th level of the previous season or, even more commonly, from having been worse than 20th in the prior year. Twenty-two of the 50 instances (44 percent) of the best players were likely not even worthy of being a second wideout for a fantasy team in the previous season.

If there are two common themes, they would either be a team with a poor rushing game that was forced to throw, and/or the wideout found himself as the only truly viable target for the quarterback (see Appendix, Table VII). Most often that comes from an injured player missing time but it can stem from a team that loses a good wideout to free agency or retirement and no other wideout steps up to fill the void. That leaves just one good wideout behind,

WHERE WIDE RECEIVERS ENDED THE SEASON BEFORE THEIR TOP 5 YEAR

Ended	Top 5	6th–10th	11th–20th	>20th
1997	0	1	1	3
1998	1	0	1	3
1999	1	2	0	2
2000	2	0	0	3
2001	4	0	1	0
2002	3	0	0	2
2003	2	0	2	1
2004	1	0	3	1
2005	0	1	0	4
2006	1	1	1	3

Figure 9.3

who becomes a great fantasy player for the year. You have to find the situation where one wideout is clearly favored by the quarterback, who has almost no other options.

While the top five wideouts each season typically had 44 percent (about 2) players shoot up from 20th or worse in the previous season, that phenomenon happens even more in the next tier of sixth to 10th best. The reason is easy enough to discern—the top five witnesses a select few players who repeat (Randy Moss, Terrell Owens, Marvin Harrison, and so on) each season while the rest of the NFL is far less consistent. Consider in the ten-year sample in figure 9.4, 27 of the 50 instances of a player ending up sixth to 10th best came

WHERE WIDEOUTS ENDED THE SEASON BEFORE THEIR 6TH TO 10TH PLACE RANKING

Ended	Top 5	6th–10th	11th–20th	>20th
1997	2	1	1	1
1998	1	1	1	2
1999	0	0	1	4
2000	1	1	1	2
2001	0	2	2	1
2002	0	1	0	4
2003	1	0	0	4
2004	2	0	0	3
2005	1	1	0	3
2006	1	1	0	3

Figure 9.4

from having been worse than 20th the previous year—over half. These players are all difference-makers for fantasy teams and a great deal of them came relatively cheap in a draft that year.

This grouping typically comes from three categories (see Appendix, Table VIII). There are possession receivers who will gain a bit more yardage but primarily they just happen to catch an unusually high number of touchdowns that season. Then there are several who experience their breakout season anywhere from their first to third year in the league. Lastly, there are a number of players who experience the magic year, the season where it all comes together like never before or again.

BREAKOUT YEARS

There is perhaps no term more lovingly used by fantasy fans than "breakout year": the season that witnesses a player leaving the mass of average receivers and turning in what appears to be a defining notice to the league that he is the newest member in the elite receivers club. While too often the players expected to break out will just break down, each season contains several who will greatly benefit their owners. The notion that a wideout always breaks out in his third season has some credence but actually does not even describe most players (see Appendix, Table IX).

Since wide receivers sometimes start notoriously slow or even play sparingly in their initial season, the best measurement is how many full seasons they have played. Taking a sample of 17 players (see Appendix, Table IX) who either were already at the top of their position or who have recently had a breakout season during a two-year span, only five of them experienced their first big year during their third season. Slightly more common was the fourth season, and there were four who had their first big year occur in just their second season.

All but one did so with the team that originally drafted them, and after their fourth year as a full-time wideout, only one had the breakout year come later. It either happens in their first four seasons or it never does. Muhsin Muhammad was an extreme exception to the rule.

As a rule of thumb, it is most often players in their third OR fourth season as starters who experience the breakout season. It can happen at other times but the majority of players break out in their third or fourth year.

ROOKIES

Recall that running backs most often had a breakout season as rookies and that almost none stepped up big after their second season as a full-time player. Now forget all that for rookie wideouts. It just does not happen. Yes, Randy Moss had 1,313 yards and 17 touchdowns as a rookie. It was beautiful. It was great. It never happened before and likely won't happen again. Get over it. Marques Colston turned in 1,038 yards and eight scores in 2006. Another decade and maybe another rookie wideout may matter in fantasy football.

Most fantasy fans love rookies and the unbridled optimism and potential they bring into the league. You can get them relatively cheap and, until the season begins, you can easily pretend you have the next Randy Moss. Go ahead and imagine you're dating a Hollywood starlet and winning the lottery as well. Now wipe that smile off your face: From 2000 to 2005, there was only one rookie wideout who ranked better than 23rd and only two others who were 24th or better—not too impressive (see Appendix, Table X).

Only Michael Clayton, Andre Johnson, and Lee Evans had any significant fantasy value as rookies since 2000. Other than Clayton, they were only worthy of being a third-ranked wideout for a fantasy team. They come cheap—but all too often, not cheap enough. The bang for the buck is just not there.

Sure, the allure of a rookie wideout is undeniable. They catch everything thrown at them in training camp. They sign huge dollar contracts and come off amazing college careers. And then they spend their first season making their fantasy owners slap their foreheads, muttering "What was I thinking?"

DRAFT PLANS

Your first consideration in drafting wideouts is their relative value as shown in a LAG analysis. They are more difficult to draft because of the variation year to year of almost all players outside the elite handful. And yet most leagues require there to be three starters, so waiting on them as so many do usually means having a third of your starting roster taken from a group of players who are already notoriously hard to predict.

The best bet is to ensure that you have at least one productive, highly reliable wide receiver. Not a player coming off a freak high year and not a rookie or someone who is anything less than a primary wideout for his NFL team, and who can be relied on to produce at least moderately consistent fantasy points each week. The best fantasy owners will aim to include a mixture of wideouts that includes a couple of possession receivers, at least one or two players in a breakout scenario, and as many top players as can reasonably be acquired without undue harm to other positional needs.

It is important to recognize the wideouts who come off an uncharacteristically big year that cannot reasonably be repeated. Each season over half of the top wideouts will come from deep in the draft and yet over half of the players who had great seasons will fall significantly the next season. Look for the talented players first, and then consider those situations that indicate a breakout could occur—lack of rushing game or a player spending the season with very little competition for passes.

Understanding wideouts and projecting them well is the final sign that you are at The Next Level. No other position produces as much empty hype each summer as does wide receiver. Take the ones that look the best for this year, not last year.

TIGHT ENDS

"There are two kinds of tight ends. Playmakers and 'just tight ends.'"

EVERY NFL TEAM has tight ends. In the average year, around 100 of them will record at least one catch in the NFL. At least two per team and sometimes up to four will have action during the season. And yet there is no ball-handling position so devoid of fantasy-relevant players. The reason is simple enough—there are tight ends who block and there are tight ends who receive. Some do both. And none of those really matter either. The few tight ends who have significant fantasy value are not really tight ends—they are playmakers.

For a tight end to become a stud, he needs a bit more to happen than any other position. While quarterbacks primarily most need situation, running backs must get the opportunity, and wide receivers have to possess that extra talent, the reality for tight ends is that they require two main qualities to be a true playmaker.

Rule 11

TE Value = (Talent × 2) × (Situation × 2) × Opportunity

Obviously, all positions need opportunities to post fantasy points, but every offense will have at least one tight end on almost every play. While growing in importance in the NFL, by no means do most offenses use their tight ends to catch many passes. And that requires not only for an offense to be willing to throw more to a tight end than most teams, but for the game situation to dictate that a higher volume of passes is required, whether from a need to score or a chronic third-down problem. Lastly and yet just as important as the other two, the tight end must be a talented receiver. In years past, you could not only count the number of fantasy-relevant tight ends on one hand, you always had at least a free middle finger to flip at all the nonrelevant fantasy starters.

There is some very good news inside of this—conventional wisdom says that tight ends are becoming more and more important in the NFL. There is a problem with that, though. It is not entirely true. Using a 1/10 yardage and six-point scoring, let's consider the top 10 fantasy tight ends during the period of time when the big change started (see figure 10.1).

Viewing those top 10's, it's obvious that tight ends really became much more involved starting around the 2004 season. The jump in fantasy points went from a total of 854 points for the top 10 in 2003 up to 1,137 points the following season. That's an increase of over 33 percent in just one season that has been borne out in following years. The tight ends have arrived! Viva la Tight Ends!

Well . . . before we make sweeping generalizations let's take a closer look. For tight ends that scored over 100 fantasy points, there were only two in each season prior to 2004. Then suddenly the number shoots up to six and then rises again to seven in 2005. But as mentioned, it is not so much about tight ends. It is about playmakers.

Using those four sample seasons, let's remove the players who scored over 100 fantasy points and see how many had between 70 and 99 points—an average fantasy tight end (see figure 10.2).

Once those top playmakers are removed, suddenly the fantasy points and other statistics no longer have a 33 percent difference. They almost have no difference, especially when taking into ac-

THE CHANGE IN TIGHT END VALUES

	2005				2004				2003				2002		
Pts	Rec	Yds	TD's	Pts	Rec	Yds	TD's	Pts	Rec	Yds	TD's	Pts	Rec	Yds	TD's
170	89	1,101	10	174	81	964	13	152	71	915	10	120	68	836	6
131	65	891	7	168	102	1,258	7	125	62	770	8	111	63	773	7
128	75	855	7	133	87	980	6	87	57	693	3	94	74	894	2
119	71	774	7	113	48	774	6	73	44	552	3	82	61	686	3
118	65	877	5	103	73	791	4	73	46	492	4	82	54	442	7
110	66	757	6	102	61	666	6	72	40	541	3	77	43	478	6
102	78	905	2	94	82	825	2	72	49	598	2	73	51	613	3
88	60	582	5	94	71	705	4	70	55	517	3	68	36	455	5
85	45	554	5	78	30	364	7	66	48	535	2	67	39	485	4
85	61	682	3	78	34	361	7	65	38	409	4	65	43	461	4
1,136	675	7,978	57	1,137	669	7,688	62	854	510	6,022	42	839	532	6,123	47

Figure 10.1

TIGHT ENDS WHO SCORED BETWEEN 70 AND 99 FANTASY POINTS

2005				2004				2003				2002			
Pts	Rec	Yds	TD's	Pts	Rec	Yds	TD's	Pts	Rec	Yds	TD's	Pts	Rec	Yds	TD's
88	60	582	5	94	82	825	2	87	57	693	3	94	74	894	2
85	45	554	5	94	71	705	4	73	44	552	3	82	61	686	3
85	61	682	3	78	30	364	7	73	46	492	4	82	54	442	7
82	39	459	6	78	34	361	7	72	40	541	3	77	43	478	6
76	55	530	4	72	25	423	5	72	49	598	2	73	51	613	3
72	37	488	4	69	36	572	2	70	55	517	3	68	36	455	5
68	47	516	3	67	37	314	6	66	48	535	2	67	39	485	4
67	29	441	4	67	34	377	5	65	38	409	4	65	43	461	4
65	55	543	2	66	29	309	6	64	46	401	4	62	27	253	7
62	68	568	1	58	28	287	5	60	40	356	4	59	34	419	2
750	496	5,363	37	743	406	4,537	49	701	463	5,094	32	729	462	5,186	43

Figure 10.2

count that differences are divided out over 10 players. Other than the top playmakers, the difference has been less than four fantasy points per player comparing the highest year to the lowest year. Over a 16-game season, that's about one more fantasy point for the average tight end *per month*. Not exactly a difference-maker there.

The influx of tight end playmakers happened for a couple of reasons. Colleges are now cranking out more pass catchers as their offensive schemes have used the tight ends more. Players that once would have just been oversized wideouts or even turned into a defensive end are now playing tight end. Players like Antonio Gates and Tony Gonzalez who used their size and speed to excel in basketball are now being featured as tight ends (though actually Gates only played basketball in college). Guys like Jeremy Shockey, Jason Witten, and Alge Crumpler are not being asked to primarily block and have receiving serve as their main role.

Another significant change is the demise of the pure West Coast offense. Starting in the 1980s, that scheme employed fullbacks and running backs as receivers while tight ends had a far lesser role. In the 15-1 season by the 49ers in 1984, their top tight end was Russ Francis, with just 23 catches for 285 yards and two touchdowns. Brent Jones had a freak high of nine scores one year but only averaged three scores per season during his 11-year career and never had more than 68 catches in a season—his average was around 40 per year. The fullback Tom Rathman had receiving production almost equal to Jones and, added to Roger Craig's numbers, invariably outperformed the tight ends.

In a league of copycats, the style of offense was distributed throughout the league as the Bill Walsh coaching tree spread its branches. But that was then. By the time we passed the year 2000, the use of fullbacks in the passing game had started to completely evaporate. And who filled in for fullbacks? The playmaker tight end. And those few great ones are doing much more than any fullback ever managed.

BREAKOUT YEARS

Before we consider the concerns and adjustments to projections for tight ends, we have to first recognize that while there are many more of them now than in past years, there still is not enough to grant studs to every fantasy team in your league. Since they are relatively rare compared to other positions, knowing when they break out into being a stud is critical.

While most wide receivers break out in their third and fourth seasons, *the surprising fact is that stud tight ends typically experience their first big year in their second season* (see Appendix, Table XI). A few needed three full seasons and only Marcus Pollard required four years (and thanks solely to playing with Peyton Manning). Using that sample as a key, tight ends usually break out in their second season. Some may need three full seasons. After that—you can pretty much write them off if they have not broken out yet.

Merely being a first-round pick did not mean that the player was destined for greatness. Antonio Gates, Marcus Pollard, and Jermaine Wiggins were never drafted. Shannon Sharpe came very close to being undrafted with his less-than-lofty 7.27 draft pick back in 1993. Those top players came from all over the NFL draft boards in April, if in fact they were even on any team's list.

ROOKIES

Now, knowing that tight ends hit the big time so very early in their careers, it makes the average fantasy fan salivate at those incoming rookie tight ends, hoping for another Jeremy Shockey equivalent. And as usual, they are going to be disappointed (see Appendix, Table XII).

Jeremy Shockey had a huge rookie season with yardage (864) but only scored twice. That was good enough to rank third best back in 2002 when tight ends were still little more than Tony Gonzalez and a pack of guys you could almost pick out of a hat. Consider that Shockey's 94 fantasy points in 2002 would have only ranked him eighth best in 2005.

Other than Heath Miller in 2005, no other rookie tight end was worthy of being a fantasy starter and almost none of them even ranked well enough to merit being a fantasy backup in most leagues. Just doesn't happen in year one. Even Miller was not that great, since he scored five times in four games and then did little for the final eight games of the season. The next year may be the start of a big career, but year one is better off left alone in all redraft leagues. The hype is easy to get caught up in but the reality is that a rookie tight end is almost a lock to have no fantasy relevance in his first season.

CONCERNS AND ADJUSTMENTS

There is no big secret to which players will be the coveted tight ends every season, and your initial projections may end up almost unchanged given that a tight end is typically either a known stud in an offense that will make heavy use of him or just another name to call in a draft because you waited too long. The reasons to change your projections for tight ends make for a short list:

1. **Coaching Changes**   Incoming coaches bring new offensive schemes. If a stud tight end already exists, it is almost certain that his role will remain because he is a playmaker, not "just a tight end." The only truly interesting aspect here is if the incoming staff has a reasonably reliable track record of using a tight end in the passing game. Even then—the talented player needs to be there already.

2. **Wide receivers**   In order to expect an increase in tight end receptions in an offense that has not undergone a change in scheme, there has to be either a significant reduction in the quality of receivers (increasing the use of the tight end) or a notable increase in talent of the wideouts (which decreases the use of a tight end for at least the number of receptions and yardage).

3. **Track Record**   As previously shown, if a tight end is known to have talent and is entering his second or third season, take a long look at how likely he will be for turning in a breakout season. That has to incorporate all three elements—opportunity, situation, and talent—before you can reliably assume a breakout is likely. Tight ends who were highly successful receivers in college are rarely drafted to become an extra blocker on the offensive line.

DRAFT PLANS

As always, performing a LAG analysis will indicate what the relative value of a tight end is against the other positions you will be drafting. While having a top player in every position is certainly a ticket to the championship, obtaining bang for your buck is paramount in assembling an optimal team. If there are no reception points, typically tight ends will not score much more than a #3 starting fantasy wideout. If reception points are included, the value of those playmakers rises dramatically.

Best bet for tight ends is to review some mock drafts to gain a good idea of where tight ends are being taken (as long as they closely resemble the scoring and starting rules of your particular league). The good news for tight ends is that there are many more playmakers now and the question is no longer if you pick Shannon Sharpe or Tony Gonzalez early or wait until the end to get your player from the heap of mediocrity. With six to eight (or more) good options at tight end, you need to determine how long you can wait and still get optimal value from the position without losing more points for your team by skipping another position.

PLACEKICKERS

"Picking a fantasy kicker is like going with a buddy to a bar to pick up women. You know that even if you get first pick, you're going to spend the evening talking about cats and ex-boyfriends while your buddy scores."

WHAT IS HARDER than drafting a placekicker? NFL teams often treat them as if they were merely a piece of equipment, and their fantasy value is both hard to forecast and of small consequence. The problem with kickers is that their production is tied to factors that are less reliable and more challenging to predict consistently. The conceptual equation for a kicker varies significantly from all other positions.

Rule 12

PK Value = Opportunity

While talent has a major role in all other positions, it is much less a characteristic to search for when evaluating kickers. Sure, there are always a few kickers that will shank their way out of a job, even in deep leagues. With the average fantasy league only requiring 10 or 12 starting kickers each week, there will be only about a third of NFL starters used in fantasy leagues—easy enough to avoid those bad kickers.

The talent of a kicker is twofold. They must be clutch kickers who can nail the game-winner on the final play of the game while 70,000 fans at the stadium are screaming for them to miss. That is pressure. And that really does not have much significance in fantasy football. It's just one field goal in question—maybe two or three over a season. The other measure is how accurate they are with their kicks. But accuracy (the ratio of field goal success) versus attempts is hardly indicative of how many points a kicker will produce in a season.

Consider figure 11.1, which shows a five-year sample for the top 10 most accurate kickers each season and where they ranked in total points for the year.

The most accurate kicker has done well in some cases. But considering that there are typically only 10 or 12 starting kickers in a fantasy league, at least one of the top two most accurate kickers each season had no fantasy relevance. In some cases they are not even worth much as a replacement for a player on bye week.

TOP 10 KICKER ACCURACY RANK (FG%) VS. TOTAL POINTS RANK (1–32)

	1	2	3	4	5	6	7	8	9	10
2006	4	11	10	19	2	12	1	17	22	6
2005	2	20	23	6	17	3	11	12	7	31
2004	1	11	8	13	4	6	9	17	27	2
2003	2	22	1	7	11	21	5	6	29	3
2002	28	8	3	2	9	25	12	5	20	4

Figure 11.1

TOTAL POINTS FOR TOP 10 KICKERS EACH SEASON

	1	2	3	4	5	6	7	8	9	10
2006	143	136	131	121	119	117	116	116	115	115
2005	148	140	131	125	121	121	117	117	115	113
2004	141	129	124	122	122	120	119	117	117	114
2003	163	157	134	125	123	120	120	114	114	112
2002	138	133	130	128	128	128	120	117	117	115

Figure 11.2

Accuracy is important in the NFL, but on fantasy teams it has little relevance overall as a predictor of points.

The reality for kickers is that not only are the points produced the only important criterion, but the bang for the buck of having a top kicker is much less than seen in other positions. Looking at a five-year sample again, the reality of kickers comes to light (see figure 11.2).

Really the only kickers of any consequence are the ones who score at least 130 points in a season. That usually only describes three kickers per year and sometimes describes none of them. Consider that the 130 point mark—rare as it is—is only about 17 points better than the 10th best kicker. That equals a whopping one point per game difference on average. One point can win your game to be sure, but that only happens when you are fortunate enough to actually have a top kicker. Forecasting them cannot be done by virtue of their talent. Another natural assumption is that the highest-scoring offenses produce the best kickers. It seems reasonable, but while there is some benefit from having a kicker that consistently scores each week, the highest-scoring offenses are not necessarily going to produce the best kickers.

TOP 10 KICKERS FOR EXTRA POINTS VS. TOTAL POINTS RANK

	1	2	3	4	5	6	7	8	9	10
2006	2	20	1	10	18	5	21	9	12	16
2005	13	6	12	3	8	4	1	5	9	19
2004	7	12	10	1	6	9	18	2	4	5
2003	12	7	8	16	1	2	5	9	11	6
2002	9	5	6	2	1	7	11	10	14	3

Figure 11.3

Consider figure 11.3, which shows the top 10 kickers from a five-year sample in kicking extra points—a true measure of a high-scoring offense. For each of those top 10 kickers that year, consider where the kicker ended up in total points that season.

In most cases the top kicker had only average value as a starter if in fact he produced enough to warrant being a starting kicker. High-scoring teams were well represented with a top 10 kicker of extra points never falling below 20th best in total points—but as a reliable indicator, it's only mildly worth considering.

The average fantasy team owner will use the previous season's stats for kickers as their main key but that often disappoints as well. While their last year will seem to be the most reliable indicator of the current season's likely success, kickers as a whole are just unreliable from year to year; even in the case where they are a top scorer, the difference between a top kicker and an average fantasy starter is often minimal.

Using the average draft position for a five-year sample from all leagues at MyFantasyLeague.com, compare the kickers' draft position against their actual ranking in total points that year.

FIRST 10 FANTASY KICKERS DRAFTED VS. WHERE THEY RANKED FOR THE YEAR

	1	2	3	4	5	6	7	8	9	10
2006	7	12	9	16	11	20	30	13	22	3
2005	19	6	30	9	27	7	11	25	3	8
2004	7	24	5	2	1	8	6	27	11	21
2003	9	25	6	21	24	2	15	10	7	19
2002	17	22	7	2	4	5	11	6	8	3

Figure 11.4

Only about five of the first 10 kickers drafted end up worthy of being a fantasy starter and all too often the picks completely flop. Consider the track record of the first two kickers drafted in most leagues over that five-year period. Only once were they better than an average fantasy starter and half of them were outright busts. Amazingly, many of these kickers elicited "nice pick" comments when they were drafted. They just are not reliable overall and they have minimal difference when they do end up on top.

So is there anything that can help target which kickers have at least the highest probability of being a fantasy starter? It is not talent. It is not being on the highest-scoring team. It is obviously not the previous season that sends the highest-scoring kickers to the top of draft boards the following season. Drawing back to the equation—there is one factor and that is all about opportunity. How can that be measured?

It is a combination of extra points and field goals that produces the total points and we know that extra points alone are not a reliable indicator of total points. The field goals are where the difference is mainly made and think about what a field goal really is. An offense moves down the field successfully but then stalls somewhere between the 35-yard line and the end zone. A field goal attempt is merely the end product of a semi-successful drive and even then the game situation can force the team to use fourth down in an attempt to keep the drive alive or score a touchdown. A team may also be trying to run out the clock and happily accept a safe drive that ends with a field goal rather than risking a pass for a touchdown. There are a number of reasons why a team would want to try a field goal and just as many ways that a team could find itself in field goal range.

A field goal then is not a "proactive" play; it is merely a "reactive" result of a particular drive. The most reliable factor in determining how often a kicker will be in that position is to rely on the historical amount of opportunities that a team gives their kicker. Remember—it's not really about the kicker as an individual player. It is about the number of opportunities that an offense produces. While most teams vary from year to year, there are those teams that are either consistently good or bad. Those good teams are the ones that offer the highest probability of getting a starter quality kicker. Those worst teams are ones to avoid, regardless of who the kicker is (see Appendix, Table XIII).

Jason Elam in Denver has never been the best kicker. But he has also never been worse than top 10. The same has historically held true in Indianapolis, Pittsburgh, Philadelphia, and Baltimore, other than one bad year for each team. Those teams had the same coaches and same offensive scheme during those five years and that produced top kickers almost every year. Consider the case of Kris Brown. He was the fourth best kicker in the league in 2001 while with the Pittsburgh Steelers. In 2002, he went to the new Houston Texans and has been mired in placekicker poverty ever since. He is no less talented. He just plays for the worst team in producing opportunities for kickers.

DRAFT PLANS

Each season will produce a few kickers with notably more points than the rest, but even in those best-case scenarios the difference in most leagues ends up about one point per week. And that is if you could actually forecast those kickers who will be getting an extra five field goals over the course of the season than the rest.

The best course of action is to maintain knowledge about which teams are consistently producing top 10 kickers. All you can reasonably hope for is to increase your odds of drafting a starter quality kicker and that doesn't necessarily have anything to do with the previous season or a kicker's accuracy or if he kicks indoors. It is all about opportunities that are afforded to the kicking game by the offense.

Those "nice pick" kickers are most often disappointments regardless of how good it feels to see the top kicker from the previous season on your roster. Remember—you are drafting a team for this year, not last year. Determine which kickers offer the lowest risk of ending up top 10 and then wait as long as you can to get one. Anything earlier than that is just a wasted pick.

DEFENSES

12

"If I only knew now, what I'm gonna know then . . ."

SELECTING A FANTASY DEFENSE often happens at the end of the draft and for a good reason—like placekickers they are notoriously difficult to get right. The kicker gains his fantasy value as the end result of a series of downs that ends inside the opponent's 35-yard line. He kicks a field goal. Kickers vary because it all depends on a factor outside themselves—how well the offense moves the ball without actually scoring a touchdown.

Defenses are hard to forecast in fantasy terms because their value is derived from a collection of 11 players who are reacting to what is happening on the field. Their success factor, much like that of a kicker, is dependent in part on something they do not control. Each opponent will bring in a unique set of players on offense who will follow a game plan and then react to the game situation. In that way, each NFL defense is also predicated on their own offense since that has a major bearing on what the game situation is.

This chapter is very short for a good reason—you could write an entire book on defenses and consider just the fantasy scoring rules in your particular league. There is no fantasy position that has such wildly varying scoring rules as the defense (which most often includes special teams). In some leagues, they are the lowest-scoring position and in others they will rival any other position in importance. It all depends, and that is exactly why this book began with the tool you should use—a League Analysis and Graphing.

Many and possibly most fantasy defenses only award points for sacks, turnover recoveries, safeties, and touchdowns scored by the defense or special team. The problem in forecasting which teams are going to be the best to draft is that those categories are among the most unreliable from year to year. Great defenses will excel in those actions, but considering that most defensive scoring ends up with little variance outside the top three, top teams are difficult to predict. A great year will stem from having the best schedule against teams that allow the most points (from throwing interceptions, allowing sacks, and so on) and there could be a change in the offense from that NFL team, which means the defense will not be playing in as many advantageous situations the following year.

Some leagues add in elements of holding down rushing and passing yardage with bonuses or penalty points associated with certain thresholds. Those are better indicators of how good a defense is and allow a defense's track record to matter more than merely with turnovers and sacks. Other leagues introduce bonuses or penalties for the amount of points allowed by a defense, which is more easily forecast but is also more contingent on the schedule that year. It's all rather complicated in the end and it can only be uncovered by performing a LAG on your fantasy league to determine just how valuable defenses are in your scoring. If they are not particularly valuable and you will only gain one point per week on average by owning the very best defense, then it likely makes little sense to be in a rush to make the first guess.

The best bet is to run a LAG on your league and then review the defenses at the top to determine what characteristics they had the previous year to land them there. Were they also the #1 defense in the NFL in terms of yardage allowed? Did their special team scores really boost their fantasy value? If defenses are significantly higher-valued in your league than most, then a deeper review of their per game scores from the previous season can show if one wildly successful game skewed their season results.

How reliable will those previous season stats be? Consider figure 12.1, which highlights the year-end rankings for defenses in 2003 using the standard defensive scoring for sacks, turnovers, safeties, and touchdowns (the teams are listed in order of how they ranked in their third year).

HOW DEFENSES RANKED FOR 2 YEARS BEFORE AND AFTER SAMPLE YEAR 2003					
	1	2	3	4	5
NE	4	10	1	3	29
STL	6	22	2	30	9
BAL	19	9	3	2	20
KC	30	13	4	20	22
TEN	24	11	5	21	17
MIA	11	15	6	26	7
MIN	31	32	7	23	4
SF	17	27	8	28	13
DET	26	14	9	12	17
CAR	12	5	10	9	1
ATL	25	6	11	4	15

	1	2	3	4	5
TB	8	1	12	14	13
GB	3	2	13	24	27
SEA	16	16	14	13	9
NYG	20	25	15	15	3
PHI	9	3	16	16	24
IND	21	28	17	5	5
PIT	7	8	18	8	6
OAK	15	7	19	32	31
NO	14	4	20	10	32
DAL	27	17	21	31	24
BUF	29	31	22	1	19

	1	2	3	4	5
DEN	13	21	23	29	9
WAS	23	19	24	22	15
CLE	1	20	25	25	28
CIN	18	30	26	6	8
NYJ	5	26	27	11	20
CHI	2	24	28	7	2
JAC	22	23	29	27	9
ARI	28	29	30	18	23
SD	10	12	31	19	26
HOU	—	18	32	17	29

Figure 12.1

Two thousand four undoubtedly had the draft order look suspiciously like the year-end rankings from 2003 in most leagues. And yet 2004 saw only two teams—the Patriots and Ravens—return as being worthy of a fantasy start. Remember, all we really care about is the number of defenses that will be needed to start in your league each week. Pretty bleak, eh?

None of the top three teams from 2002 returned to the top 12 in 2003. The top three teams from 2004 again had none return to the top 12. Using the basic scoring of rewarding sacks, turnovers, safeties, and touchdowns by the defense or special teams ends up with wildly varying results from year to year and is almost impossible to rely on in terms of burning an early pick.

That all said, notice how many of the bad defenses remain bad. This typically happens when a defense not only has an obvious lack of playmakers, but also from that team likely having a poor offense. While it is difficult at best to correctly target which defenses are going to be best in your fantasy scoring, at least tagging the ones that are locks to be bad is much easier.

Lastly, there is one common strategy used in fantasy football that bears commentary because it extends to all defenses no matter what the particular fantasy point rules are. How many times have you heard—or even said yourself—"I'm not going to grab an early defense, I'll just swap out weekly if I have to play match-ups"?

Having seen that so many times and tried it personally, this strategy spawns an important rule:

Rule 13

DEF Value = 80% Talent + 20% Match-ups

You can chase all the great match-ups you want but if your defense has few playmakers, it's not going to matter. The game score may remain low and your defense may be on the winning team, but in most leagues you are not going to profit nearly as much as just owning a very solid defense. Every season there are typically two or three teams that are horrible for whatever reason and those will very often give up nice points to opposing defenses. However, those truly bad teams do have the occasional good game and the reality is that they are not going to be facing a team on your waiver wire every week. When you get a truly great defense going against a truly bad team, good things are going to happen for you. But when you take an average defense and hope to get anything similar, chances are high you will be disappointed.

Grabbing a great match-up on occasion can make some sense, don't misunderstand. But planning on doing that weekly is fraught with peril and disappointment too often to make it an attractive strategy in almost all cases. The bottom line is that there will be many weeks where all the bad offenses are facing defenses held by the rest of your league.

Again, the area of fantasy defenses is quite complicated by the tremendous variation in how different leagues score them. Use a LAG and understand just what their value is in your scoring and how they match up against other positions. Look at what sort of defenses did well the previous season and then look for defenses that share those same characteristics for the next year. And know that it won't always be the previous top scorers and, in many years, it won't be any of them.

SECTION

III

YOUR **Fantasy
Draft**

THROW YOUR
PROJECTIONS AWAY

13

"Projections are no substitute for judgment; they merely assign a number to what a player may produce based upon previous years that will never happen again."

PROJECTIONS ARE THE LIFEBLOOD of understanding players and creating rankings. They are a must for any serious fantasy football team owner to create. And once they are recorded, adjusted, pored over, reasoned, compared, and adjusted again, they are ready for the important step of being applied to your league's scoring system in order to find the fantasy points per player in your league. Sort by position and descending fantasy points and you have instant rankings! Woo-hoo! Where do I sit at the draft?

Well, hold on there, Sparky. This is just the point in time that you can throw away your rankings. Or at least set them to the side. Understand that those projections have now served their main purpose—to create an ordered list of players AND hopefully to help you learn a bit about each player along the way. True enough, there is draft software out there to make the process just a simple keyboard click from projections to creating rankings. Looks great, and some software applications are incredibly slick. There are even various statistical "systems" to use to further complicate the process of determining which player to take in your draft, and they all use those wonderful projections.

Before you consider these options, recall one thing—a League Analysis and Graphing will already show you what the scoring is going to look like in your league this year: It shows the relative values between players using actual statistics from your last fantasy season. To create rankings, projections are critical to create and apply to a fantasy scoring scenario, but let's play a little *Truth or Consequences* here and see what three options we have with our projected rankings:

1. **Do Nothing**   Not only are you draft-ready, but you have some nifty-looking rankings that actually change when you alter the projections. Oh look! One fewer touchdown and he dropped 13 spots!

2. **Use a Player Value System**   Fun with math time! Using a player value system that relies on projections to further evaluate and consider players is like betting on an inside straight in poker for every player considered. You could be right, but is it really worth betting on every time?

3. **Door #3**   Aka The Next Level.

DO NOTHING

For those of you who use projections for creating rankings and stop with that, let's consider what projections actually are. They represent what analysis and research suggest is the most-likely-case scenario for a player. That sounds like a good thing. But every player has a vast number of potential endings to their season and all your work has predicted only one of them. The effects of injuries, team dynamics, individual game situations, and a multitude of other factors are all going to come together and result in what a specific player will produce in a season. This results in our next rule:

Rule 14

Projections, by their very nature, only describe one potential outcome.

The difference in projected fantasy points from player to player is not going to be 100 points. It may not be more than a point or two. You may even end up with a clump of five players all with the exact same projected fantasy points. Realize too that projections invariably have players ranked much closer to each other than what actually happens, as almost all players are projected to play a full season while there are rarely more than perhaps 10 running backs and 15 quarterbacks who play all 16 games in a season.

Missing games contribute much to spread out the actual stats of NFL players but in the scenario of projections, one extra touchdown could move a player up half a dozen spots or more. This means that you are valuing one player to be five slots more desirable than another player on the basis of one possible play during the season. Top quarterbacks are involved in over 500 pass attempts and runs each season. Top running backs will have over 350 carries and receptions each year. You must be rather proud of those projections.

USE A PLAYER VALUE SYSTEM

Most player value systems started in fantasy baseball—a sport that produces statistics over 162 games. There you have a player with known ability performing over and over during the year and way down the road ending up with a season statistic. It doesn't matter if he misses a dozen games. It probably doesn't matter if he spends two weeks trying to convince a congressional committee that he bulked up using Flintstones vitamins. He has 162 games to play.

But in football, there are only 16 games in a season. Considering that most leagues start the playoffs in week 14, your projections must be successful for the first 13 games during the season or they don't really matter. Only 13 games—not 162. Even if your "most likely" projection ends up close to reality, it doesn't matter much if the bulk of the points all came in the final weeks of the season when you are out of the playoffs.

Player value systems consider that the projections are so correct, further manipulations of them will determine the best player or position to draft. A simple LAG graph already shows the relative value of positions in your unique league scoring. Comparing positions to each other using projected statistics must also somehow take into account position scarcity, the potential of runs on a position, the possible necessity of reaching the player's backup before anyone else can, and a host of other considerations that do not lend themselves to a nice, neat number. If you just want to stick with numbers, the Japanese puzzle game Sudoku may be more to your liking.

There are a number of very successful fantasy football players who ascribe to one style of player valuation or another, if in fact they have not created one for themselves. I would strongly contend that their success is not because of a value system per se, but because of everything they have done up to the point of projections. Let's sum it up this way. They spend a tremendous amount of time in analysis and research to create their projections and then apply a player valuation system to them to bring the projections to yet an even higher level of reliance. But if you know anyone who uses those systems or if you personally rely on them, ask just one question:

"Do you always pick the highest-ranked player on your sheet for the entire draft?"

THE NEXT LEVEL

The answer you should get is "no." They do not rely purely on their projections or what player their valuation system suggests is the best choice. Just to test my theory out, I polled 68 veteran members of The Huddle with a simple question and the response merely confirmed what I already knew.

WHEN DO YOU DEVIATE FROM TAKING THE HIGHEST-RANKED PLAYER ON YOUR CHEAT SHEET?		
Almost never	[0]	[0.00%]
Only in final rounds	[3]	[4.41%]
Only after mid-draft when I am picking backups	[5]	[7.35%]
About the 6th to 8th round	[5]	[7.35%]
About the 4th to 5th round	[3]	[4.41%]
3rd round	[0]	[0.00%]
2nd round	[1]	[1.47%]
Rankings are only guidelines; I can deviate at any time	[51]	[75.00%]

Figure 13.1

Exactly 75 percent of them said that their rankings are only guidelines and that they can and will deviate at any time. About 90 percent of them had deviated before they were finished selecting their starting roster and the remaining 10 percent left their rankings only in the back half of drafts, likely because of bye week needs and to avoid loading up on a single NFL team for their fantasy roster.

So all that work goes into projections, and many fantasy players even further manipulate those predicted fantasy points into player valuation systems, yet the vast majority of them are not using those rankings for any hard-and-fast decisions? I'm actually surprised it was not a little higher. This is because projections are never more than guidelines, something more related to tiering groups of players than assigning a hard-and-fast draft slot.

You must create projections to better understand all the NFL players and then apply that knowledge to create your statistically validated rankings. And those rankings array the players one by one in the one potential ending for their season that you believe is most likely given the tremendous number of potential outcomes. And at that point, numbers have served their purpose. Trust me—I love numbers and crunching statistics. But they can only provide you with one thing—the most likely outcome over an entire noninjury season that ignores how it is accumulated during the season or how likely that outcome really is. Two players could have the same projected stats and yet Player A could have "I would bet my wedding ring on it" probability while Player B may only be "Well, this is about as good a guess as any" kind of player.

What The Next Level does is to take all the great qualities of statistical projection to create your cheat sheet rankings and then apply considerations that do not lend themselves to numerical expression despite being every bit as important. Yes—you need to rely on your projections as being the most likely outcome and therefore the only one that matters to you. But you have to rearrange those rankings using your personal judgment.

REASONS WHY PROJECTIONS ALONE ARE INADEQUATE FOR RANKINGS

1. Reliability

2. Risk

3. Upside

4. Consistency

While fantasy football is obviously a hobby rooted in the statistics produced by NFL players, the athletes are not automatons performing a mechanical process (no matter what some NFL owners believe). As with any human competition, there are a variety of influences that affect the outcome that do not lend themselves to a tidy number system. Using projected stats is a nice start to creating rankings, but it should never be the final step. Not when there are four major components of player ranking that lie outside the realm of best-case season total numbers.

RELIABILITY

While two players may have identical projections, the reality is that often one player can be relied on more to produce than another. Fantasy fanatics love players that offer consistency from season to season. If the projections for one player are for 150 fantasy points for the third year in a row, those are fairly reliable. If another player projects for 155 points but comes off just 50 points in his rookie year, he is more worthy of drafting than the 150-point player?

If there is one aspect that fantasy team owners love, it is drafting a "sleeper." Having a player that follows a quiet season with a major production increase the next year is often the ticket to a championship, given that you were likely able to draft him well below his actual value. The problem is that everyone is trying for the exact same phenomenon; within the beauty of the Internet and its ability to disseminate information is that it is too often just baseless hype. This leads us to one very important rule.

Rule 15

Overreaching for an "upside" player is the most common mistake.

This is true for first-year fantasy team owners and the most veteran fantasy team owners alike. Reliability is critical to consider when deciding between two players. Every player has their "right spot" to be picked and there is no truly "undraftable" player (at least given unlimited roster size). The hype each season for third-year wideouts and rookie runners (to name but two) often propels them higher in projections, and therefore rankings, than is warranted. The reliability of a player takes greater importance since you should be drafting a player in their appropriate draft spot. This is not to say that you should stock up on aging veterans, by any means, only that you must take into account the reliability of your projection before you draft one player over another with a similar projection.

When looking over your rankings, ask yourself, "Just how reliable is this player to meet my most likely stat projection?"

RISK

Risk is the other side of the reliability coin. It involves not only how likely your projection is to happen but also what the most likely worst-case scenario will be. It is easy enough to consider what a player's ceiling might be for the upcoming season but what is his floor? If he misses the mark of the projection, just how far can he fall? Like reliability, which considered how likely the projection is to occur given the past track record, risk considers just how far off that projection could likely be.

Risk is another consideration for each player within a grouping of similarly projected stats. The summer can help fan the flames of hype, but realistically just how far can a player fall from what was considered the most likely outcome? Rookies carry a tremendous risk. Players who have notable injury histories also carry the danger of falling well short of expected production. Some risks pay off and most don't. That can be addressed by selecting a player in the correct slot during a draft provided no one else has overvalued him. Another common mistake is to overvalue the chance that a player will take over a starting role that he does not have in week one.

Some risks are worthwhile, but when reviewing a player in your rankings, always ask yourself, "Is there a reason why this player could do significantly worse?"

UPSIDE

While reliability and risk give solid reasons why a player should be ranked lower, the aspect of upside promotes reasoning why a player may be valued higher than the projected rankings. This applies much more the lower you go in your positional rankings. Obviously the top players will have little upside, but those middle and lower tiers should be adjusted by considering what the ceiling could be for the player. While not as important as what you have determined as the most likely outcome, when all things are equal—always take the players with the greatest upside.

Upside is created when a player has a realistic chance at taking over a starting role for the first time or when the team dynamics have changed in such a way that favors the player. The more veteran a player is, the less upside he is likely to have unless significant changes have happened to his team for the first time in his career. In a sense, all players have at least some upside but those who have a significant chance to outpace your projection are the ones to consider. Should you shoot a player up the rankings because he has a chance to really break out? Not if his risk and reliability balance that out.

For each player you consider drafting, ask yourself, "How reasonable is it that this player could significantly outpace my projections?"

CONSISTENCY

Player consistency is something that I stumbled across about 15 years ago. Back in the days when the weekly scoring was conducted by the guy with the box scores and a spreadsheet, there was almost no access to just how consistent a player was from week to week. But while projections are made for a season total of statistics, the way that players gain the stats made a significant difference. Remember—those first 13 games of the season mean everything to your fortunes as a fantasy team owner. This is not baseball, so there aren't 162 chances to even out all the numbers. There are only 13 games in the average league regular season that combine to determine who the best head-to-head winners are who will advance to the playoffs. Your fantasy team is much better off with a player who can score consistently from week to week than it is with one who has numerous big and small games. Think of it this way: Would you rather get 10 points per week from a player or three-week sets of 22-5-3? Figure 13.2 is a real-life example of three wide receivers during the 2005 NFL season who could mirror projected stats in total points.

YOUR FANTASY DRAFT

SAMPLE PLAYERS FANTASY POINT CONSISTENCY			
	Player A	**Player B**	**Player C**
Total Points	153	152	150
10+ Points	8	5	9
<6 Points	3	1	0
1	24	32	18
2	5	8	20
3	20	12	B
4	3	23	10
5	11	7	13
6	20	6	17
7	13	B	6
8	17	5	16
9	B	9	11
10	11	7	10
11	9	15	8
12	18	14	15
13	4	14	6

Figure 13.2

While arrayed in total points as would be with projected rankings, the consistency factor says the actual value order is wrong. Player C may have scored fewer total points than the other two players, but he had the greatest number of games of 10 points or more (nine) and he had no games that fell below six points. Player B only had one game of fewer than six points but also only had six games with 10 or more points. Player A scored more total points than the other two and yet had more games (three) when he scored fewer than six points in a game. His healthy eight games counterbalance those three bad games.

Considering the above scenario, the most valuable player would have been Player C because every week he was above six points and remained over the 10-point mark more often than the others. He was rock-solid. Player B was not so much bad as he was not all that great from week to week. Player A weighed in with a nice number of big games but tossed in a few clunkers along the way.

Consistency applies to all positions, to be sure, but with wideouts it becomes the most exaggerated. Your projections should have initially considered the consistency of a player and as a last check should be weighed again on your final rankings. I've carried consistency rankings on The Huddle since 1997 because it is a valuable tool in understanding not only what players produced overall the previous season, but how they went about creating that season stat. Undoubtedly there are teams in your league that will vary from being the highest-scoring team to the lowest from week to week because their players are inconsistent—feast or famine. And riding those waves usually lands you around .500 for the season in won/loss. Even if you have to do it yourself, you should be aware of the consistency of a player and then use that as a consideration in final rankings. In random match-ups for head-to-head leagues, the best you can do is to remain above average every week. That means consistent performance from your players.

Those four factors—reliability, risk, upside, and consistency—are factors that should greatly influence the choices that you make in your drafts. The fact that 75 percent of the people in my poll may deviate from their own rankings at any time is a reflection of their use of judgment over statistics. Those four factors are usually inter-related and are present to some degree for every player.

Rule 16

True player value considers
reliability, risk, upside, and consistency.

TIERING: STEP UP TO A
BETTER DRAFT

14

"It's all friendly until there's just one piece of pie left."

HOW MANY TIMES have you been in a draft with plans to snag a prized player only to see him taken with the pick before you? Hurts—doesn't it? Never mind that you have not been looking at any other players while waiting, you now have to do something and fast. What to do? Waste time pining for the player who was just selected or go find a new one?

If you've followed along with my suggestions and concepts, there is no doubt that you have a very solid set of rankings. They've been created on three years' worth of stats and considered the common elements of sleepers and breakout players. You know which positions are more valuable than others at any given draft pick and you've used your reasoned judgment to adjust those projection-inspired rankings with the nonqualitative considerations of reliability, risk, upside, and consistency. By now you will have the best possible set of rankings you could have possibly created. All that's left now is to print the rankings out and bring a pen to the draft, right?

Well . . . maybe just one more step.

You are finished with your rankings but what you have left is to make up a cheat sheet—that very document that you will be zealously guarding with your forearms every time someone walks behind you at the draft. After you have arrayed each position into their order of best value, the final step is to create visible tiers within each position. The reality with a draft is that your league will use perhaps six different fantasy positions and perhaps nine or 10 starters per week. If everyone would just agree to raid one position at a time, then yes—rankings alone would be enough. Since that is not going to happen (besides perhaps a running back frenzy in the first round), each team is going to be considering the various positions they need to fill each time they draft. Because players from each position will be taken throughout the draft, you need to tier.

Tiers are made by determining which players are relative equals in what they can deliver this season. A tier should contain players that "net out" the same when risk and reward are considered. A tier may contain players who are the product of projections or just personal preferences, but a tier contains a group of players who you would be about as happy with no matter which one you took. They are all ranked in order for selecting, but tiers offer a much better way to address the hectic pace of a draft.

To be sure, tiering is an art form.

Before delving into the art, there is a bit of the science behind the concept of tiers to look at. In fantasy football, each season will produce approximately the same scoring from season to season in any given scoring scenario. The actual stats themselves fall into tiers because there are players who score similarly to one another, and yet there are small groups that represent a step down from the higher tier and a step up from the lower tier.

Tiers occur naturally (see Appendix, Table XIV). Normally, three players in each position will top the lists each season. Some years only have two and occasionally there will be four, but around three players generally make up the top tier in any position. These are the annual superstars, the major difference-makers who likely delivered more than a few fantasy league championships.

The next tier is made up of players who may not be the very best, but were all rock-solid starters in your league. After that group, tier three steps down to the more average athletes. And so on. It can be different depending on the scoring system used, but there is always some amount of consistency to naturally occurring tiers. Within any position, there will be clumps of players who will score in a smoothly declining fashion, then a noticeable bump down, then a more gradual decline. Your tiers do not need to match the previous season's natural tiers since each season does not exactly repeat.

WHY CREATE POSITIONAL TIERS?

Tiering is just establishing groups of players who you view as similar enough that the best and worst in that tier carry relatively the same risk/reward. That depends on subjective determinations, which are nothing more than what projections are anyway.

Tiers allow you to better address your own needs compared to what players are available. Basically, tiers can build a better team during the portion of the draft where starting positions are being filled, and in some cases can help determine if you should grab a running back or backup quarterback or take your first tight end or defense or whatever.

Drafts rarely meet expectations on how particular players and positions are taken. You can plan ahead, based on your draft slot, as to which player or position you are going to target. I have personally done that in probably every fantasy draft I have had since 1995. I can also claim that I cannot ever remember actually following the plan in its entirety in any draft. Why? Because there are no two drafts that are exactly alike.

You must know what values are still on your board at any given moment. There will always be a run on the running backs in every draft given their value, but the use of tiers allows you to know if the time has come to go grab that quarterback or wide receiver. Typically, I have always preached taking quarterbacks later—perhaps the fifth or sixth round. However, there are the occasional drafts when the running backs are flying off the board so fast that by my second pick I am still looking at a tier one quarterback or receiver.

Tiering makes it easier to see where value picks are still available. Those are the ones that yield a big advantage. You can glance at your tiers and see where the greatest value lies when your turn arrives. All drafts should be about gaining the greatest overall values for your team to produce maximum points, and tiering makes that feat much simpler. Tiers allow you to see how deep each position is and how quickly others are draining.

Tiering also allows you to quickly recover from the #1 tragedy in any draft—the one guy you wanted the most gets picked right before your turn. Inside your head you may be screaming about how close you came to the steal of the draft but no one really cares. You can even announce the old "that was my next pick!" but everyone pretty much assumes you forgot about the player until someone else picked him.

Tiering makes your rebound easier. You can assess the remaining players more easily and quickly knowing what small groupings you have to choose from, how many of the same-tier players are left, or where other value may exist in another position.

Creating positional tiers allows you to effectively manage the draft and thereby the flow of optimal players onto your roster. It also helps you to track the draft, change course, and recover quickly from having your big sleeper snapped up right before your selection.

HOW TO TIER

Tiering is an art that allows you to control your drafting or auction process. While you could create your own tiers based solely from projections, and many do just that, tiers should be created considering groups of players that offer similar risk/reward. For example, you may have a tier that contains some solid yet unspectacular players and mix in some potential superstars that have unusually high risk. However they come together, you consider each player in that tier to be effectively the same. More importantly, you consider the final player in that tier to be a definite step-up from the first player in the next tier.

To provide a simplistic example, here's a sample of how to view building tiers within a position.

Tier 1 The high scorers of the previous season who have minimal reasons why they will not repeat. These are the stud boys who no one should question and who everyone wants. Tier one should consist of around three players.

Tier 2 The high scorers from the previous season who have reasons why they may not repeat, but who even in the worst case should be solid enough. As close to a superstar as you can get.

Tier 3 Solid performers who offer a low risk of a bad season and yet with an upside for a big year. These are usually either the average starters for the position or a player with such a significant upside that you are willing to accept greater risk in exchange for a much higher ceiling on what they may produce.

Tier 4 Solid performers who are either great players on the downturn in their career or high-risk/reward players.

You can make your tiers even more useful by taking the average projected fantasy points for that grouping and writing it between the two tiers:

USING TIERS WITH AVERAGED POINTS TO GROUP PLAYERS IN POSITIONS

Quarterbacks	Running Backs	Wide Receivers	Tight Ends
322 pts	**375 pts**	**305 pts**	**230 pts**
1 ~~Peyton Manning~~	1 ~~LaDainian Tomlinson~~	1 ~~Chad Johnson~~	1 Antonio Gates
2 ~~Tom Brady~~	2 ~~Larry Johnson~~	2 ~~Steve Smith~~	2 Jeremy Shockey
3 Carson Palmer	3 ~~Shaun Alexander~~	3 ~~Torry Holt~~	3 Todd Heap
290 pts	**275 pts**	4 Terrell Owens	**160 pts**
4 Eli Manning	4 ~~Steven Jackson~~	**260 pts**	4 Alge Crumpler
5 Matt Hasselbeck	5 ~~Tiki Barber~~	5 Randy Moss	5 Tony Gonzalez
6 Drew Bledsoe	6 ~~Edgerrin James~~	6 Anquan Boldin	6 L. J. Smith
7 Marc Bulger	7 ~~Ronnie Brown~~	7 Larry Fitzgerald	7 Jason Witten
8 Donovan McNabb	8 ~~Clinton Portis~~	8 Marvin Harrison	8 Heath Miller
9 Aaron Brooks	9 ~~Carnell Williams~~	9 Reggie Wayne	9 Chris Cooley
10 Jake Plummer	10 ~~Rudi Johnson~~	10 Donald Driver	**100 pts**
11 Trent Green	11 ~~Willis McGahee~~	11 Roy Williams	10 Ben Watson
12 Kurt Warner	12 ~~LaMont Jordan~~	12 Darrell Jackson	11 Bubba Franks
260 pts	13 ~~Brian Westbrook~~	13 Derrick Mason	12 Randy McMichael
13 Michael Vick	14 ~~Domanick Davis~~	14 Chris Chambers	13 Vernon Davis
14 Brett Favre	**200 pts**	**220 pts**	14 Dallas Clark

Figure 14.1

YOUR FANTASY DRAFT

Placing the average point values for the tier above each grouping gives you an easy and immediate way to compare two positions. Using the sample cheat sheet, consider if it were your turn to pick. You could see at a glance that you can either take quarterback Carson Palmer with a 30-point advantage over the next tier, or grab wideout Terrell Owens for a 45-point difference, or go for the first tight end in Antonio Gates with a very hefty 70-point advantage over the next tier. Just to remain realistic, the running backs are already taken well below the 200-point level and would have to be evaluated on the basis of how many remained in the next available tier.

Tiering beyond the number of starting spots per position has much less benefit. Even when it comes to wideouts, there is usually no real reason to go beyond four or five tiers. But for those early rounds, placing the average fantasy points of that tier in a visible spot gives you more information to make a good decision when you draft. It makes comparing the best available players much quicker. A glance tells you not only the point values you are expecting from certain players, but also just how many players are left in each tier and, therefore, the probability of still being able to snag players from the grouping if you wait until your next pick.

APPLYING YOUR TIERS

Tiering players allows for quick decisions that are supported by your previous research and thoughts. When your pick comes up, you can easily review the remaining players in sets of tiers rather than by specific player names. If you see that only one player remains in, say, tier three for running backs and yet there are six left in the highest open tier for receivers, you immediately know that you can take that runner and still get as good a receiver with your next pick while the running backs would surely be gone at that point.

The safest way to tier is to make a top three in each position be tier one; then tier two would normally be about five to eight players. Tier three is about the same number of players. You have to incorporate the tiers into your draft strategy knowing the relative scoring value of your positions. The size of a tier is entirely related to the net value of all grouped players, considering risk and reward.

The greatest advantage you can have in a draft is the ability to build the optimal team by taking players who are the best available and yet fit into your needs for starters. Particularly in rounds two through seven, using tiers allows you to "see" your draft as it unfolds and as positions are raided. It is far more effective than becoming mired in comparing projections for individual players across positions, because you do not often have the time to do that when the draft is underway. You have to be able to make a quick decision that is the right one and, of course, drafts never unfold exactly like you thought.

Tiering is every bit as valuable for auctions as well, since player value is paramount. There is no need to spend huge sums of salary cap dollars on one player if there are a couple of others still available and who could be had for less money. You save in one spot to spend in another. Tiering cannot make up for bad player rankings, but it can turn good rankings into gold.

Apply tiers in at least one of your drafts to see just how much faster it becomes to determine the best available when it is your turn to pick. Using the average point values makes the tiering even more informative and valuable during the hectic pace of the draft.

One of the worst and yet most common events in a draft comes when that one player you want very badly ends up taken right before you pick. Two months of secret plotting and planning have just landed in the trash can thanks to the bozo with a cheat sheet to your left. And the clock is ticking.

What are you going to do?

MOCK DRAFTS ARE FANTASY
FANTASY FOOTBALL

15

"You rotten, lying son of a bitch. That was MY pick . . ."

(My friend Bob Scheckman, during the 2004 CoolBear Invitational draft)

THOSE WORDS WERE SPOKEN to me during the second round of a fantasy draft. Actually, to be more accurate, Bob uttered a string of expletives using only a few connecting verbs and the repeated use of the word "mother." You see, his problem was that he had the pick right after mine and he too had targeted Terrell Owens. He was rather certain he would get him for a very good reason—mock drafts.

Not just any mock drafts either. During June, we often would hold the first eight rounds of a 12-team mock draft over the phone (nice practice, actually). We would divvy up six teams each, pick one as our personal team, and faithfully draft the other five to see what the league would look like with different strategies. He had no inkling that I wanted Owens mainly because I would never draft him in any of the half dozen mock drafts we held. I just did not want to tip my hand and I also wanted to see where Owens would eventually fall. I later reviewed our old mocks and noticed he had done the exact same thing. I was so sure he did not want him, I almost waited until my third-round pick, but with another team between us, I did not want to risk it. My fondest memory of that season will always be grabbing Owens and watching Bob go nuclear. Ironically enough Bob later beat me in the league championship in part because I was missing an injured player—Terrell Owens.

But for those half dozen mocks we had, I always selected a running back in the second round even though I knew I wanted Owens there. Bob had occasionally taken a wideout in the second round but it would always be Chad Johnson as a ruse. The point of this is that there are many positive aspects to participating in a mock draft or even just viewing those of others. But they do have certain limitations that must be recognized. Rely too much on mock drafts and the results can be frustrating, if not disastrous.

WHAT'S BAD ABOUT MOCK DRAFTS

Because mock = fake. Trying to glean any highly reliable information from a mock draft is like pretending that those Lamaze classes were the same thing as childbirth. It all takes a different slant when your wife actually tries passing a moderately sized watermelon through the equivalent of Coke bottle. It is also different when teams are taking players they are actually going to rely on for an entire season. Sure, there may be more pain involved with the childbirth, but mess around with Bob's next pick and there's about the same use of colorful language.

Mock drafts by their nature are not real. They are just a pseudo-realistic way to try out different strategies to see what works best while likely most other mock drafters are doing the very same thing. It does not matter if you are having a mock draft with your best friends or total strangers—people love to play around in a mock and act in ways that will often be different from when they actually have to pick players. Drawing any hard-and-fast information from them is just not going to prove highly reliable.

Rules are rules. Before even bothering to view a mock draft, make sure that you understand the scoring and roster rules. This has a major bearing on where positions are drafted. The most important factors to look for are the presence of reception points (which increase the value of third-down backs and possession receivers, as well as devalue running backs relative to receivers), the points awarded for a passing score (making the quarterback more or less important), and the number of starters for each position—particularly the presence of a flex player, which will often make running backs go even heavier in early rounds as teams try to attain three starters.

The initial three rounds of drafts will usually not change dramatically with different scoring and roster rules, but the next four rounds are where their differences are most felt. After the first three players are taken for each team, the drafter is making largely strategic decisions based on what he still needs and believes will best address the rules.

Mock drafts are from a different time. Unless you are reviewing a mock draft that was started and completed earlier during the day of your draft, you are looking at players picked during a different time. Players get injured, developments alter starting roles, and a host of other factors happen daily during training camp that impact the value of players and can even affect the value of positions as they compare to each other.

Consider that most of those mock drafts you see in magazines were conducted in May, when rookies were brand-new and unseen on their new teams and considerable changes had yet to occur—players may even move to different clubs prior to your purchasing the publication. Check the dates of those mock drafts you are reviewing because time is everything. The older the draft is, the less reliable it will be.

To provide an example, consider figure 15.1, which shows the average draft position for the first 60 picks (five rounds in a 12-team league) from mock drafts completed in July versus those at the end of August. This sample comes from 2004 but could be any season.

WHERE INDIVIDUAL PLAYERS WERE DRAFTED IN THE FIRST 60 PICKS BETWEEN JULY AND AUGUST

	1	2	3	4	5	6	7	8	9	10	11	12	13	14	15	16	17	18	19	20
July	1	3	4	2	7	5	8	11	12	10	15	19	6	14	9	20	21	16	17	20
August	1	2	3	4	5	6	7	8	9	10	11	12	13	14	15	16	17	18	19	22
Change	0	-1	-1	2	-2	1	-1	-3	-3	0	-4	-7	7	0	6	-4	-4	2	2	-2
July	21	22	23	24	25	26	27	28	29	30	31	32	33	34	35	36	37	38	39	40
August	13	18	23	25	26	24	27	28	33	32	29	36	30	60	54	38	31	41	35	37
Change	8	4	0	-1	-1	2	0	0	-4	-2	2	-4	3	26	19	-2	6	-3	4	3
July	41	42	43	44	45	46	47	48	49	50	51	52	53	54	55	56	57	58	59	60
August	40	45	34	67	55	49	65	44	84	39	51	46	43	52	50	62	66	57	70	58
Change	1	-3	9	23	10	-3	18	4	35	11	0	6	10	2	5	-6	-9	1	11	3

Figure 15.1

Consider too that the movement shown in those averaged mocks already had the advantage of averaging, which makes player movement in a draft less pronounced than in any individual draft. While the first 33 picks had minimal changes, where players fell after that point changed significantly in just one month. Those later rounds are the ones where you are looking to add strategic backups and sleepers, and knowing when you can get them is paramount to developing a sound draft plan. Unfortunately, the older a mock draft is, the more movement happens where players are taken.

The average draft position maximizes the bad. One of the most beloved tools by many fantasy football fans is the averaging of mock drafts, real drafts, and even rankings from multiple sources. As we have seen, unless the drafts were very recent, there is variation in each that is smoothed when averaged. Those changes that caused the movement of where individual players were taken are mixed in with any drafts from a time previous to the change, so important movement becomes hidden by averaging a number of drafts.

Unless the scoring and starting rules were exactly the same between all drafts—highly unlikely—it also washes out the differences that exist when there are significant rule variations from draft to draft. For some changes, like reception points, it can affect not only how positions are drafted relative to each other but also where individual players are taken, because their value goes up or down in relation to the change in scoring.

Just as significant, mock drafts contain a lot of player choices that would not be made in a real draft, as mock drafters try different strategies or try to cloak what they really want. Fantasy team owners who rely on mock drafts to get the average draft position for players (which can then be turned into an average set of rankings) will most likely draft an average team that has an average season. Averaging mocks and real draft results often washes out the best information and sets yourself up for missing players because someone in your league will want each coveted player more than the average person.

Before you settle down with your first fantasy football magazine or online draft results, make sure you follow one of the most important rules in this book. If you have to break rules, ignore all the others before you ignore this one:

Rule 17

Never view any rankings until you are finished with your own.

This includes mock drafts, since they are a de facto set of rankings assembled by the actions of a group of people. Your rankings must contain what YOU believe about players because only you are going to live with the results of your draft. All your research, analysis, and fact finding go into your projections and subsequent rankings that should be adjusted with sound judgment based on reliability, risk, upside, and consistency. The last thing you want is to influence that with the actions of a couple of jokers in a mock draft or by the rankings of some other person or Web site that slaps them up in early May by tweaking last year's stats.

This is very important for two reasons. Once you have established what your thoughts are on all the significant players, you will undoubtedly discover that you are higher on several players and, unlike many other people, you will have a knowledgeable, valid reason for believing what you do. Those are the players you most want to track through the summer because they are good value players you can take later in your drafts. Call them sleepers or undervalued players, but those guys will be your ticket to a better team. Don't let the perceptions of others impact your beliefs before you are certain what you personally believe.

On the other side of the coin, there will be several players who end up drafted much earlier than you value them. If you are in an auction league, those are the guys you throw out first to let the others burn up excess cash on players who you do not value nearly so high. In a draft, you need to be aware of who those players are so you can reasonably guess where they will go and what more desirable players will still be available for you.

Viewing mock drafts and other rankings *after* you have your own rankings provides a nice checkup on where you see players valued. There is a chance that some of those "too high" and "too low" players from the mock draft will cause you to rethink what you have, and that is fine. Make changes to your rankings when you are alerted to something you may not have realized or weighted properly, but don't ever buy into simple hype or unrealistic downplay. Fantasy players at The Next Level may be wrong occasionally, but they are never in doubt. Make up your own mind—don't let someone else do it for you.

WHAT'S GOOD ABOUT MOCK DRAFTS

While mock drafts have some major limitations, they are still wonderful tools when used in the proper manner. Viewing the first mock draft of the season is always one of the most fascinating events of the year. You have your own rankings and opinions and finally get to see how closely your thoughts align with others. And each subsequent draft you see can make your rankings and draft plans better.

Mock drafts show where players are GENERALLY being taken. While you can never rely on your draft matching up player to player with any mock draft, chances are pretty good they will have many similarities. Mock drafts are a way to see how other fantasy team owners are valuing players. Granted, you must consider the scoring scenario used and when the mock draft was held—but after spending so much time by yourself projecting and ranking players, it is a great way to see how your rankings are likely to fit into a draft, where the good value players are, and how you can build an optimal team of starters.

The best-case scenario is to find about three mock or real drafts that use a very similar scoring scenario to your league and that was held within a week or so of your draft. Then don't average them—review them individually for where specific players are being taken. When there are players that you want, the important fact is not where they are being taken on average, but what the high and low picks are on them. From that you can glean when you need to select a player with a realistic chance of reaching him. If a guy is your super-sleeper, then you must know the earliest he has been taken in similar drafts and be prepared to grab him no later than that point.

Mock drafts display the relative value of positions. This is where even older mock drafts still contain value. Forgetting about individual players, it is imperative that you know when and where the various starting positions are being drafted. There is no magic player who will make or break your draft, and so long as you can determine where positions are being raided, you can compare that to your tiers to determine how early or late you must make your move to acquire a player from a specific position and still get the desired value.

While running backs will always fly off the shelves early in drafts, the biggest value of similarly scored mock drafts is where the quarterbacks, wide receivers, tight ends, and even defenses are being taken. This should at least resemble what you will be seeing in your draft. This knowledge is critical in determining where you can grab that starting player and still access the tier that you want. If mock drafts provide nothing else, this one aspect makes them worthwhile to watch.

An interesting tack to take with mock drafts—as long as they are reasonably similar in scoring and roster rules—is to just de-

DRAFT POSITIONS OF FIRST 12 QUARTERBACKS DURING 3 MOCK DRAFTS

	1	2	3	4	5	6	7	8	9	10	11	12
Mock #1	2.11	4.03	5.01	5.08	5.12	6.02	6.07	7.03	7.04	7.07	7.09	8.08
Mock #2	2.06	4.09	4.11	4.12	5.03	5.09	6.01	6.05	7.05	7.06	7.11	8.03
Mock #3	2.06	4.09	4.10	5.04	5.07	6.01	6.02	7.03	8.05	8.10	9.02	9.04

Figure 15.2

lete the names and then view the positions as they were drafted. Consider the samples of where quarterbacks were drafted during three mock drafts in 2006 (see figure 15.2).

The consistency in all three drafts equates to decent reliability. While the first quarterback taken (Peyton Manning, of course) went from the middle to late second round, the next one was not taken until well into the fourth round. If I have my sights on the #3 quarterback, I know I need to take him by the end of the fourth round but there should be no need to worry about it in the third round. If I believe I can live with the 10th best quarterback, then I wouldn't worry about drafting him until around the seventh round while mining the other starting positions until that round.

Once again, there is some consistency in how this position was raided in three different mock drafts. There was the first player taken (Antonio Gates), who always went on the turn in the third round. Then the next one would not be taken for about another full round. If I really want a top three tight end, I had better plan on getting him by the mid-fourth round, though he could last a little longer. Settling for a top five player meant setting that fifth-round pick to the side for my tight end. I may even get lucky and get the #4 tight end there depending on when I pick.

FIRST 8 TIGHT ENDS DRAFTED IN 3 DRAFTS

	1	2	3	4	5	6	7	8
Mock #1	3.01	4.02	4.04	5.06	5.07	6.09	6.10	7.05
Mock #2	3.02	4.05	4.10	5.01	5.12	6.02	6.06	8.04
Mock #3	3.02	4.06	5.03	5.09	5.10	7.01	8.03	8.06

Figure 15.3

Aside from that sort of refined planning is using the mocks to measure how many players in a position can reasonably be expected to be gone by your pick. Consider what those always coveted running backs did per round from that sample of the three mocks in figure 15.4.

While there was some variation from round to round, I can look at my tiers and know that I will likely need to grab my two starting running backs by the end of the first three rounds or I will be using a player that is probably not in the top 20, since all three drafts had 21 running backs taken in the first three rounds. After the eighth round there is no chance for anything better than the 40th or worse back remaining and I know from my LAG analysis just how pitiful the scoring is at that point.

That LAG analysis is a great way to compare similar mock drafts even if you just keep the knowledge in your head and don't commit it to paper. While most people look at mock drafts and just see names, playing at The Next Level means you know that the information about how positions are being drafted is every bit as important as anything you are going to glean about an individual player.

RUNNING BACKS DRAFTED IN THE FIRST 8 ROUNDS

	1	2	3	4	5	6	7	8	Total
Mock #1	12	3	6	5	2	4	4	5	41
Mock #2	11	6	4	4	3	4	5	5	42
Mock #3	12	5	4	5	3	3	5	4	41

Figure 15.4

Mock drafts reveal how the first five picks can build teams.

While the mantra of "pick the best available player" is thrown about drafts, the reality is that everyone is trying to build a team that will feature the best roster possible from which to pull their starters. Those first five picks provide the core of your players and cull out your share of the top 50 or 60 NFL players. After those are secured, you are either filling holes or shoring up depth. Mock drafts give you a great way to see how different strategies play out in the draft.

The standard start to any draft is likely RB-RB-WR-WR-QB or RB-WR-RB-WR-WR or some minor variation. By the end of the fifth round, most teams will have either two running backs and three wide receivers or three backs and two wideouts. Inserting a quarterback or a tight end into that mix has a significant effect on the other starting positions. Viewing how well individual teams use different strategies yields useful information for your own plan. That early quarterback often leaves a significant downgrade at running back and that early tight end usually means the starting wideouts take a hit. With a mock, you can see what plays out and what you may be able to get away with in your own draft.

This is particularly interesting when you know your draft slot and can review several mocks for what happened to others who were picking from the same spot as you. While the names you pick will be different from the mock, you can expect to see a similar result if you use the same plan as the mock draft at that draft slot.

Mock drafts are fascinating to view and are crucial to review before making any draft plans. The information is there, at least in a general sense, and can be a tremendous help in building your optimal team. Just don't get too set on grabbing the next Terrell Owens in the second round of your next draft.

NAVIGATING YOUR DRAFT

Lt. Colonel Bill Kilgore: You either surf or you fight.

(From Apocalypse Now, *1979)*

AH YES, CHRISTMAS IN AUGUST. The most anticipated day of the year for many fantasy fanatics, and before they ever walk in the door, they need to know—are they going to surf or fight? Are they going to create a realistic game plan that allows them to build an optimal team while being prepared for any surprises or are they just showing up to pick names off a list and hope they get to their favorite players before anyone else does? Drafting at The Next Level is all about preparation and the ability to respond to the unique path that every individual fantasy draft will take. You can either be the guy who is surfing through the draft or the one dodging bullets wondering why you enlisted.

If you've followed The Next Level steps, before you pick your first player you have already:

1. Performed a League Analysis and Graphing (LAG) to better understand how players are valued in your league and how the positions relate to each other.

2. Created your own set of projections based on previous season total statistics and the previous year weekly statistics, which were then adjusted after taking into account the variables that affect the different positions.

3. Created your own set of rankings that takes those re-searched and reasoned projections and applies some Next Level wisdom to each player about their unique reliability, risk, upside, and consistency.

4. Created a cheat sheet that applied tiering to your rank-ings to group players with similar values together for an easy way to consider the remaining depth in any position instantly.

5. Reviewed at least a couple of mock drafts with similar scoring systems that have been held as recently as pos-sible.

By now you are like a master fisherman, loaded with state-of-the-art rod and reel, a tackle box full of the perfect lures, and a map of the lake. All that is left is turning that masterful cheat sheet into an actual team. Just one challenge remains—everyone else has the same objective and they will be standing there elbow to elbow with you casting their hook into the same pool of players. You can crave a surefire, guaranteed superstar player but if he is taken before you can pick him, it doesn't matter what you wanted.

Drafting a team is not like picking winners in a horse race. Each player only goes to one team and everything you plan must accommodate the fact that you will not get every player that you want. Is it really possible to screw up your entire draft by seeing one player get selected prior to your pick? Probably not. Remember—you can fight or you can surf. And there is a tool to ensure that you land as many of the players that you possibly can to create that optimal team.

THE ADVANCED DRAFT TRACKER

Back in the days before personal computers and the Internet made life easier, every fantasy team owner would record the player name from each pick on a sheet of paper. That way he could see what the other teams looked like as the draft progressed. One sheet would be considered the official listing after the draft was over. Now that it is the twenty-first century, is it really necessary to continue to write down each player as he is selected? No.

All you need to know is what positions have been drafted by which team—that's all. Anything more is just a waste of precious time.

Does it really matter who has T. J. Houshmandzadeh or Daunte Culpepper? Your cheat sheet already shows that they are taken—what more do you need? The only pertinent information to you is how many quarterbacks are gone, who still needs a tight end, when backup players are being taken, and so on.

TM	*1*	*2*	*3*	*4*	*5*	*6*	*7*	*8*	*9*	*10*
QB				X						X
RB	X	X	X	X	X	X	X	X	X	X
		X	X	X	X	X	X		X	
WR	X	X	X		X	X		X		
TE	X									
PK										
DEF										

Figure 16.1

The Advanced Draft Tracker is quite simple. It is nothing more than a list of the positions you will be drafting. Instead of places for player names, it merely has boxes where all you have to do is mark a large "X" in the position as it is taken by a team. For example, if team one picks a wideout, put an "X" in the wideout box under team one's column. If you are less dexterous or you're leading the pack in beer consumption, just fill in the box. It is not only much faster to record, it is even faster to view and use as a tool.

During a draft, you need time to determine which player you are aiming for with your next selection, how many players in each position are gone, what players will most likely be gone by your next pick, and how you might secure the phone number of the waitress. The last thing you need is to waste time trying to figure out how to fit the names LaDainian Tomlinson or Ben Roethlisberger onto a piece of paper. Keep it simple and you'll keep it useful.

Considering that this is merely a tool, there is no reason to make it extend any further than what your decision-making process needs it to be. Who cares who has a third quarterback? What is most important are starting positions and one backup beyond that. After that, you will be so deeply in the draft that there is little useful information to see since there is no pattern to take advantage of in regard to your planning. Deeper in the draft, everyone is hunting sleepers or drafting players willy-nilly. After I have drafted all my starters, even I abandon the Draft Tracker because it just doesn't matter anymore. We are all hunting backups and sleepers by then and there is nothing to gain by continuing to record anything. In fact, from the first pick of the draft onward there is only one major consideration:

Rule 18

Always pay attention to the short side of your draft slot.

Your draft position is itself a tool because it is uniquely yours and is directly affected by those teams around you—particularly the "shorter" side teams. Consider you are drafting eighth in a 10-team league. In the first round, there will be seven players taken that you never had a chance to draft. After your first pick, two teams will go twice (assuming standard serpentine drafting). By using your Advanced Draft Tracker sheet, it will be easy to track what is going on as the draft evolves and how you might take advantage of it. The closer you are to the end of a round, the more reliably you can forecast which players will likely be gone by your next pick. In figure 16.2, the "long" side has seven players making 14 picks—a lot can happen in 14 picks. But when four picks are made by just two teams, you can more accurately predict what will happen and what effect it will have on your plans.

TM	1	2	3	4	5	6	7	8	9	10
QB				X						X
RB	X	X	X	X	X	X	X	X	X	X
		X	X	X	X	X	X		X	
WR	X	X	X		X	X		X		
TE	X									
PK										
DEF										

Figure 16.2

Using the Draft Tracker, the sample table shows what the seventh team is looking at before they make their third pick. There have been 17 running backs, two quarterbacks, six wide receivers, and one tight end already taken off the board. You (again, drafting eight) can quickly break down your options:

- **Quarterback** There are only two taken so that final player in the top three is still available. But Team #10 already has a quarterback. Do you want a quarterback here? There will be no more than one taken before you go again if that—so is it that important to have #3 instead of #4?

- **Running Back** You certainly need to get one after spending your second pick on a stud wideout. The two teams that will be picking after you have a total of three backs already taken. Figure that Team #10 is a lock to take one running back here and maybe two. Team #9 already has his two starters, but he could go for three if he is a running back pig. That means up to three could be gone by your next pick. Do you really want the best available running back now, or perhaps the third best available one with your fourth pick?

- **Wide Receiver** Neither of the two teams after you has any wide receivers yet, so it's pretty safe to assume that at least one will be taken, if not up to three (knowing that team #10 should be getting at least one running back). Do you really want the best available wide receiver now or the third and maybe even fourth best available when you make your fourth pick?

Comparing your Draft Tracker to your cheat sheet gives you instant information that will help you to make the optimal pick. After you make your fourth pick, there will be 14 players taken before it winds back to you. There could be a sudden run on quarterbacks or everyone could just continue to mine running backs just because many team owners are just running back addicts. It doesn't really matter because you cannot do anything about it other than deal with the situation that greets you when they are done.

When the draft wraps back to the critical fifth round, the Advanced Draft Tracker sheet becomes even more valuable. Consider an example of what the eighth pick might face when the draft wraps back in the fifth round.

TM	1	2	3	4	5	6	7	8	9	10
QB			X	X						X
RB	X	X	X	X	X	X	X	X	X	X
	X	X	X	X	X	X	X	X	X	X
	X			X	X		X		X	
WR	X	X	X	X	X	X	X	X	X	X
		X	X		X	X	X	X		
		X				X				
TE	X									
PK										
DEF										

Figure 16.3

You went ahead and took your second running back and second wideout in the previous picks and now it is time to consider your options once again:

- **Quarterback** You still need one, and only three have been taken. But Team #10 already has one, so while there could, and likely will, be a run on quarterbacks between your sixth and seventh picks, there likely won't be more than one taken before you go in the sixth round.

- **Running Back** Five teams have already taken their third back, which includes Team #9. There have been 25 tailbacks already taken so the quality on them is risky at best. There could be one more taken before that sixth pick of yours. Either you take the top-ranked one with the fifth pick, get the next guy on your list in the sixth, or just skip them for two more rounds and pray something is left for you in the seventh round.

- **Wide Receiver** You probably still need one more starter and the two teams after you both only have one so far. It is almost a lock that each team will take at least one wideout and they could both snap up two of them. Do you really want that best available wideout now or do you get what could be the fifth best wideout with your sixth pick?

- **Tight End** There still has been only one tight end taken in this league. Since it is a starting position, you can be certain that by your seventh-round pick there will be several already drafted. You can consider a stud tight end here (relative term as that may be) or know you will likely be getting an average one in two more rounds.

- **Kickers/Defense** Those positions are untouched so far. In the event your league has some seriously wacky scoring, you could consider starting the run—but given how unpredictable they are, why bother with starting a run, particularly this early?

Given the above scenario, it would likely be best to take a running back in the fifth round and then still get a great quarterback before that run starts in earnest before the seventh round wraps back to you. Or do whatever you decide makes the most sense for your team with your scoring rules from your draft slot. With the ability to reasonably predict what those teams on the short side of your draft slot will do before you select again, you can make more rational and effective player decisions.

You only have to continue to use the Advanced Draft Tracker for however long it still offers you value in making picks. Typically that is around the eighth to 10th rounds once all starting slots are taken (ignoring kickers). While you could just make a Draft Tracker grid with only rows for starting positions, it makes more sense to go at least one backup slot deeper. This is important when you see from your cheat sheet that 10 quarterbacks are taken but the Draft Tracker says that includes three teams already doubling up on them. You are still not safe waiting on a quarterback in that scenario—three teams still don't even have a starter yet.

The Draft Tracker is the easiest, most usable form of keeping up with your draft as it unfolds. Write down every player name drafted if you like, but realize the point of a draft is not to be an exercise in penmanship for a piece of paper you likely won't ever look at again. The point is that you want to build an optimal team and save your writing skills for endorsing the championship check.

DRAFTING YOUR CORE: THE FIRST FIVE PICKS

"The race is not always to the swift, nor the battle to the strong, but that's the way to bet."

(Sportswriter Damon Runyon in More Than Somewhat, *1937)*

AND MAYBE "IT'S NOT WHERE YOU START, it's where you finish" is true. But it is also a bit misleading. Where you start in a draft has a huge impact on where you will end up, particularly since what you do first will affect what you can do later. Those mid-draft picks will definitely be difference-makers for the very top teams who extract much more value from their players than what their draft spot suggests should happen—but start out badly and it's guaranteed you will be fighting for the rest of the draft. You want to set yourself up to not only take the best players as they come to you, but to set up the rest of your draft so you can take advantage of the "best player on the board" instead of scurrying about trying to fill holes or catch up to position runs before the quality is completely drained. It is more than annoying to let very good players slide past you because you were not in a position to draft them.

Your first five picks will become your core players and should be your highest scorers each week. Figure, in a league of 12 teams, there have been 60 players drafted after everyone has completed their first five picks. The difference between the highest-scoring player and the 60th (not considering quarterbacks, kickers, or defenses) is about 200 points in a season for a standard performance league without reception points. The difference from the 60th to the 120th is more like only 60 or 70 points. Those top players count big and owning (hopefully) five of them in the right mixture is what will make the difference for you each week of the season.

Entering your draft, you should have at least an informal plan that you want to follow, if not two or three depending on contingencies like an unexpected star player falling to you from a position you were not initially considering at that draft slot. While that won't likely be a running back given their fervent desirability in most leagues, it certainly applies to quarterbacks, wide receivers, and tight ends. Many fantasy team owners have such a rigid plan in their head entering a draft that they completely ignore better values when they pass by because *they have a plan.* And nothing is going to make them deviate from it. Their rigidity in drafting is more like rigor mortis because many are going to end up dead by midseason with a far less optimal team than they could have had if they took advantage of good players sliding instead of "sticking to the plan."

A draft plan is a great tool, don't misunderstand. But it is merely a guideline. It should be considered much like projections—just the most likely scenario to happen. And just like projections, "most likely" rarely happens. Each draft is unique because it incorporates the divergent views of perhaps 12 team owners all using their own perceptions and prejudices to assemble a team from their particular draft slot. Truly the joy in drafting is to be able to respond to the changes when they occur and jump on opportunities while avoiding pitfalls. The draft should never be a dozen team owners reading the top name on their cheat sheet each time their pick comes up. Every draft plan should be reevaluated with every pick made. Your plans were created assuming certain players would be taken in particular spots, which would leave you with an ever reducing set of available players. And you know it won't go exactly the way you most expect. When lady luck smiles, it could be even better than you hoped.

You can start to make draft plans after you create your cheat sheet. First, you will consider where each of your starting players will most likely be taken by position. And while your first five players will create that critical core, it is actually the first three picks that require the most forethought—because simply enough, the fourth and fifth picks are a result of what happens during the first three picks. They are the two draft picks that should still be high-quality players, but depending on what you have and what is left, you may not have a lot of options for those two picks because you need core starters and the tiers with quality players are disappearing quickly. Those first three picks will determine whether you can grab a player that has fallen in the draft well below his value or if you have to snag a player at the end of a run before a certain position runs out of quality choices.

Grabbing the best available player is always the best course of action, but that also relies on how you define "best available." With a draft strategy in hand and the tunnel vision caused by so much preparation, it can be hard even for the most veteran fantasy team owner to recognize who actually is the best player. The reality is that we all wear blinders to some degree because we are so locked into what was determined as the best course of action prior to the draft. So remember:

Rule 19

It's a fantasy draft, not a cafeteria.

In a cafeteria, you grab your tray and get in line. You then proceed in an orderly manner through the presented salads, entrées, side dishes, and desserts until you reach the blue-haired matron at the cash register. Many fantasy team owners go through their draft like it was a cafeteria and can tell you before the draft which position they will be taking in what round. Regardless of what players are available, they have an ordered way of approaching their draft that entails a checklist each time the hairnet lady asks "What d'ya want?" No matter that certain players have fallen in the draft, they have to grab those two running backs and then whatever wide receiver they find in the third. And so on.

Sure, you can grab your fantasy tray and go through the line with running back, running back, wide receiver, wide receiver, and quarterback. You can plan on it and you can follow through on that plan regardless of the depth or quality you are getting. Most teams do exactly that. But treat that draft as a way to build your team one pick at a time, and with each pick reevaluate what your next move will be depending on what the situation is at that time—not a week ago when you were drinking with your league mates and decided "gonna be RB-RB-RB this year . . . *burp* . . ."

After those three picks, you'll need to make some decision based on what you have and what you see as likely still available to you for those fourth and fifth draft picks. While many variables are involved with player value—roster size, number of starters, scoring rules, and so on—let's consider generally what the most popular formations result from those initial three picks and what that likely means for draft strategy.

THE FIRST THREE PICKS AND WHAT THEY MEAN

- **RB-RB-RB** The classic stud RB (aka RB pig) start means you better be very good with WR and QB, cherry-picking sleepers to make up for some lost opportunity early. Unless your league uses a flex position, you probably just acquired only two starters with your valuable first three picks. This feels good to the RB-insecure drafters but it places a lot of pressure on the team in later rounds. It can strategically hurt other teams that waited on their RB2 in larger leagues. Unless your scoring heavily favors RB's or you get to use a third RB in a flex position, you probably just bought into being only average—at best—in all your other starting positions. You will now chase the runs on QB, WR, and TE and have almost no chance of getting a difference-maker there. Yes, we all love them. Yes, we all want them. But they still are only 25 percent of the starters in most leagues, if that.

- **RB-RB-QB** If quarterback scoring is significantly higher than other positions, this is often a good plan to use. Acquire your first two RB's and then scoop into the QB's before they start to decline quickly. In most leagues, this is actually early for a QB unless he is in the top three for the position. In a few leagues, this could actually be too late. Now, then—can you pick a couple of good WR's after the first 15 are gone? Unless you get a tier one QB, the value of this strategy is debatable. QB's do score a lot and in most leagues the top nine last out until the sixth to eighth rounds. Know your league and the scoring before going this route if you do not get a tier one QB. There is usually only one starting QB per team so they end up getting drafted less and later than other positions.

- **RB-RB-WR** This is probably about the best generic plan, discounting what values might drop in your draft. You start out with a solid RB corps, which is important, but then still reach a pretty good WR; you will need more than one anyway. Not knowing anything about a league or slot, this is the one I would tell a newbie to use since it is the safest one of all. Maybe not most advantageous in all cases, but the safest. Using the third pick on a WR means you should be getting a low-risk, high-reward player in a position that is always a challenge to get right.

- **RB-WR-RB** As long as that WR is a top three, this makes sense. Plenty of QB's left and you start out solid on RB with a great WR. Probably weaker than the RB-

RB-WR unless receivers are valued higher than in most leagues. Most of the time this has to entail a top three WR or be near the backswing of rounds two and three so a decent RB2 is still available. You need to know what you are doing on that RB in the third round.

- **RB-WR-WR** This can be deadly effective but only if you get a sleeper RB. You have wrapped up two great starting WR's in a position that is the hardest to get right. Good start but good luck on that RB2. You need to be pretty sure in your player evaluation skills to net a decent RB2, and you probably just bought into getting an RB3 earlier than most teams just to cover in case your RB2 does not work out. In a league with reception points this plan is much more popular and effective because then RB and WR are relatively equal and you can get three top players.

- **RB-WR-QB** This works well only when you have top-tier players from all the positions. If you do, then you are in a great spot to take the players that fell in the draft. If you got one of these wrong, you can be hurting your chances to compete. This can look great at the time but you'll need access to a pretty early fourth-round pick in order to reach an RB2 that will post at least moderate points. This is something best done when RB1 is a low-risk, high-production stud. Waiting until round four to acquire an RB2 can be fine, but you better have an ace up your sleeve when you do it.

- **RB-QB-WR** Same as RB-WR-QB but likely a bit less workable since QB's typically are available later in drafts. Likely lost some opportunities by going this route and will need to get lucky from here on out. That QB

YOUR FANTASY DRAFT

has to be in tier one and that WR better be a great one as well. Waiting until the fourth round for RB2, like above, is best done only when you have a top RB1 and the confidence you can find a suitable RB2 from the bargain bin.

- **RB-QB-RB** This is fine if your QB scoring is well above the other positions. Probably stronger if your RB1 is a big stud player since your RB2 will be from a later tier unless you have an early pick in the third round. Your WR1 will be a notch below most other teams but you'll have a better QB than most anyone else. Unless your QB's really score much more than other positions, this better have in it a tier one QB. You need to be good at finding undervalued wideouts when this happens.

- **WR-RB-RB** Starting with a top-tier WR is a decent idea if you draft very late in the first round and you can get enough value with RB's to make a solid start that can address value picks later. Normally what works best is to get that tier one WR and then make your RB picks be a mix of one solid guy and one big upside guy. You are headed for mediocrity if you are not careful with this and need a sleeper RB to hit for you. This makes more sense in leagues that only start two wideouts because you locked up a great one.

- **WR-RB-QB** As tempting as this may seem, taking a top-tier WR and following it with a tier three or four RB means you have set your team up for about average scoring so far in your first two picks. Taking a QB in the third round had better be a tier one QB, and even then chances are good you would have been better off overall waiting on QB. With the rate RB's fly, that WR and QB better be distinct advantages to compensate for a weak

RB2. This can work in the right fantasy scoring scenario but only in leagues where RB's are not really that more valuable than WR's.

- **WR-WR-RB** Consider this play to grab two tier one WR's only because you were drafting at the end of the first round and they fell. You have two great WR's in a normally inconsistent position. You can always get a QB later of some note and you just need to land one RB sleeper to make this work. Downside is that it almost never works. Feels good until you check out what your starting running backs look like. Considering that you will be deep enough into the RB depth that any player is a high risk for mediocrity or outright flopping, this can be a recipe for disaster that you cannot recover from because of the scarcity of available running backs once the season starts.

- **WR-RB-WR** I hope you are getting reception points because that is likely the only way this makes sense. WR1 needs to be a tier one guy, RB1 needs to be tier two guy, and then the trade-off between WR2 over an RB2 needs to be already known before you go this route. If there are no reception points, then you better be one Slick Sam at sleepers because you are buying a couple of need picks real soon. This is usually marginally better than WR-WR-RB, but it mostly works only when you draft late in the round so that your fourth pick will be early enough to access a decent RB2.

- **WR-QB-RB** This works best only if there are reception points or at least a scoring methodology that actually favors WR and QB and you are picking deeper in round one. I'm sorry—I hate to admit it as a receiver aficionado, but RB's are too valuable to wait on if only because of what the rest of your league is likely to do. You better know your league and scoring before hopping on this bandwagon.

- **QB-anything**   Rather than go through all the permutations, suffice it to say QB-anything only makes sense in leagues that give a disproportionate scoring to QB's over all other positions. In almost all leagues, you start only one and you can access a better than average QB several rounds later. QB's with value last longer than either RB or WR because you only start one QB. You really need to know your scoring here to make sense of it this year. Starting out with a QB means that you will either take an RB in the second round knowing that your RB1 won't be much better than anyone else's RB2 or you take an elite WR next and only complicate your RB woes. In most leagues, starting out with a QB means falling behind on every other position or having major holes in the quality of your starters.

Again—these are only general observations about most leagues and each draft slot has a unique set of circumstances to it. What works great with the first pick in the draft may be catastrophic if tried with the 12th pick and vice versa. This is another reason why reviewing individual mock/actual drafts can be so valuable. You can witness what someone else did with your draft slot and how that worked out for him. Learn from the success and mistakes of others. Average drafts show you nothing about how to build a team but individual mock drafts can grant you a view into the future of your draft slot.

Your draft slot is a major factor in determining what you can do and what sort of team you can build, at least for the initial five picks in the draft. The standard approach to drafting looks like this for draft order in the first round:

- **Top Three Pick**   Besides being one of the teams most envied (even if they do not admit it), you get to start the draft out with a clean slate and every star player open to you. You can take any "cough-RB-cough" player that you want and you get great picks with your 2/3 swing. You already have the equivalent of a "player and a half" to start with. This position is best used to start runs on positions and loading up on top-tier players in several positions.

- **Middle Pick**   Your decisions are far less set in stone than those first three drafters usually, but while you do not get the best locks in the draft, you still get a very good player in the first round and you have better access to grabbing value picks when they go past. Drafters on either end of the round almost always have to draft a player a little early or hope someone falls because there are so many picks before they go again that they cannot respond to sudden runs on positions or likely take advantage of a player who has fallen half a dozen spots lower than he should have been taken. This is the best position for value picking.

- **Final Three Pick**   This position seemingly sucks when you sit there twiddling your thumbs as the finest players in the draft are taken. Your first pick will be worse than anyone else's (theoretically anyway). But your second selection will be better than most anyone else's—and that is still when the quality is very high and the risk is still rather low. This position often produces league champions because they didn't have the luxury of taking a super back with their first pick and had to build a complete team. Like the first three picks, this swing drafter cannot respond well to sudden runs on positions but can instigate them for QB, TE, PK, and DEF. It is also the spoiler position because with two picks close to each other, it is a little easier to steal players from other teams—particularly backup players.

Approach your draft with a plan, by all means. Using your knowledge of the league scoring, the likely availability of players, and reviewing mock drafts to verify your plans can give you a stronger position when you enter the draft than the unprepared team owners. But that plan is only a guideline. Respond well to what is actually happening in your draft as it unfolds and chances are far greater that you'll also be responding to the question "how'd you draft such a good team?"

SECTION

IV

THE

Regular
Season
and
Beyond

THE NFL SCHEDULE— FRIEND OR FOE?

Two roads diverged in a wood, and I—
I took the one less defended by,
And that has made all the difference.

(With apologies to Robert Frost)

MY FIRST FANTASY LEAGUE came in 1990 when a co-worker of mine asked me to play in this new thing called fantasy football. Having been a big football fan my entire life, it seemed like a fun way to compete against a set of friends because I, like the other nine guys, was certain that my football knowledge was superior to theirs. After miraculously ending up in second place that year, I was hooked. We started a different league the next season with guys in the building where we worked and I was smart enough to know that I did not want to be the commissioner. But I did agree to be the league scorer. Thanks to computer software and the Internet, that job now is akin to being an AMC Gremlin mechanic.

But back in the day the process was entirely manual, using nothing more than a newspaper and a Lotus 1-2-3 spreadsheet. One by one, I would count up the fantasy points for each player in the league and record them in the proper spreadsheet cell, total them up, and then print up the results so that I could distribute them by hand to each team owner (hence the need to have all owners in the same building). It did not take me long to realize that I had access to information that no one else did. It also became readily apparent that certain players were exceeding expectations whenever they played certain teams. And other NFL teams were bringing down almost every player that they faced.

So starting around 1993, I began tracking what each defense was allowing and what the future schedule held for any player that interested me. And it worked. There were clear patterns and trends that were reliable enough to make predictions and projections. Each season, the strength of schedule came out, which showed the combined winning percentage of opponents for each NFL team, and that was all anyone had to judge how tough a season would be. All except for me and my ever-growing database of statistical information.

I wasn't really interested in schedule strength for teams—I wanted to know the ease of schedule for positions. I wanted to know which players would have the easiest schedule that season and which ones would be facing a greater challenge than most. When The Huddle went live in 1997, I published the very first ease of schedule, based on fantasy points allowed by defenses, and it's been copied by many others ever since for a good reason—it is a great tool in your toolbox. Not the only tool and not even the best one, but a definite consideration for every player.

THE DOREY RULE

During those years of scoring every player by hand each week and analyzing the results, I came across a revelation. I realized the advantages of playing an easier schedule and how fantasy teams would start and finish their seasons. While some teams finish strongly, invariably the better teams always have a hot start and then maintain their advantage or even improve upon it. After reviewing how a fantasy season began versus how it ended, it continually pointed at one factor that I adopted as my own:

Rule 20

The Dorey Rule:
Draft as if the season only lasted the first six weeks.

Those initial six games are critical to win because those will set you up for the rest of the season. Let your players struggle through a tough opening stretch of opponents and suddenly you are 2-4 and hating life. Feast on a great early schedule and being 5-1 feels pretty damn good—and you will likely be describing just how good to anyone who cares to listen. Those first six weeks are the magic mark that will define your season.

This is for many reasons. Player injuries begin to affect teams more starting in the seventh week as the season starts to wear on players. Bye weeks are underway and immediately change the makeup of starting lineups. Players who begin hot often do so thanks to an easier schedule and those too often don't last the entire season. Predictable performances last more often to that mark before the dynamics of a team begin to change in ways that could not be forecast.

There are a variety of reasons that six weeks works out as optimal, but none so compelling as having compared all the other sets of weeks during the last two decades and finding that six weeks is the magic mark. You do well in your first six weeks, you will be primed to coast to the playoffs. And those are the weeks that are the most accurately forecast before offenses and defenses start to gel and injuries begin to change up the dynamics.

Aside from the advantage of a nice season record, being a league leader after six weeks means that you can more judiciously trade away players likely to fade and acquire players likely to rise. You can take more waiver wire speculation picks on players that may pan out later because what you have has been playing well for the first six weeks. Disregard a tough opening schedule and you'll too often fall behind in the standings. That leads to desperation and poor bargaining position. It leads to making moves to get players who must contribute immediately with lesser concerns about what they may do in a few weeks, because if you do not start winning now, the later just doesn't matter anyway.

No roster remains the same throughout the season, and the injury bug bites everyone to some degree. A hot start to your season is just the biggest advantage you can give your team and will have positive effects in all that you do. Each week of the season you will be using players that have the best combination of innate talent, situation, opportunity, and SCHEDULE. Why not make the schedule part as good as it can be?

If you take nothing else from this chapter, take to heart the Dorey Rule. Even if you never touch a spreadsheet or look at statistics, at least eyeball the opening six weeks for each team and decide which teams appear to have the best and worst schedules. Once you complete your haul of the studs in the first three rounds or so of your draft, start using the Dorey Rule as a consideration when drafting a running back or quarterback and even allow it to be a minor consideration for receivers if you are truly torn between two players. I have used this concept since the early 1990s and have been publishing it on The Huddle since 1997. Of all my statistical breakdowns and analyses, the Dorey Rule has consistently spawned more "thanks for helping me win my league" than any other single offering.

It is yet another of my creations that has been copied in magazines and Web sites, and for a complimentary reason—it works.

THE EASE OF SCHEDULE

Everything up to this point has been about understanding your team. How the players have value, how they fit together to make a team, and how to continue to refine your projections and rankings so that you can be confident in what you expect of your players. Only one consideration has been missing. Whoever you draft is not going to accumulate fantasy points for your team on a practice field or on your handy spreadsheet. They are going to play in actual games. And not all games are equal, by any stretch of the imagination, because no two teams have the same schedule. Not even close.

You will know by mid-April what the NFL schedule for the current year will be. This is more than a guide to bye weeks, this is the road that each player is going to take to reach the end of the season and, hopefully, deliver your team to your league championship. In the sense of all things being equal, why wouldn't you want your players to play against the easiest possible schedule (better said, the schedule that causes them to score the most points)? While every fantasy team owner from novice to expert relies on the schedule each week of the season to make starting decisions, playing at The Next Level means that the schedule is just as important during the summer when you are making draft plans.

Before we consider the NFL schedule and how it applies to player drafting, it's important to be up front with our next rule:

Rule 21

The top players in each position are bigger than their schedule.

In essence, for elite players there is no major reason to consider what their schedule is because they are going to play well no matter who they play. During the season, this translates into "Always start your studs." Case in point—Peyton Manning has been the most productive quarterback over a number of years and in many of them he had a terrible schedule. Didn't matter—he was Peyton Manning. Same goes for Tom Brady. Same goes for the top running backs, wideouts, and tight ends. There is one small caveat we will get to later, but as a basic rule you can pretty much ignore the schedule for the top five or 10 players in each position. No need to overthink it.

However, unless you are incredibly shrewd or are playing in a six-team league, chances are you won't have more than one or two of those top players. Once you leave those elite players, the next rule kicks in:

Rule 22

The schedule is bigger than the average player.

This is just a reality. If you have two similar running backs and Player A is playing against the #1 rushing defense in the league while Player B is facing the #32 rushing defense—which one would you want to start? What applies to a single game also applies overall to the season. How many times has a player had an unusually productive year when he faced a light schedule only to drop noticeably the next season when he did not have the benefit of the schedule? How many teams made it deep in the playoffs only to flop the next year when their schedule toughened up? The schedule controls just how hard or easy it will be for each player to produce fantasy points, and it pays big dividends to know in advance of the season what to expect.

Having done this sort of analysis in each of the last 15 seasons, I will make an admission here. The ease of schedule does not really apply to wide receivers or tight ends. The problem here is that each NFL team will use at least two wideouts in each game, if not four or five. A very soft schedule will not translate the same to all receivers. The primary wideout will always get his share unless playing against an elite cornerback (if even then), but all secondary receivers have more variables involved than just the schedule. Passing is hard enough to predict since most teams will prefer to run when they can and pass no more than necessary. Passing is largely a function of game situations, and expecting there to be any reliable information gleaned from the schedule takes much more wisdom than mathematics to see how the schedule may affect wideouts.

For the same reasoning, tight ends are not worth comparing to the schedule because there are only about 10 or so each season with significant fantasy value, and those are going to be your league starters. NFL offenses are using the tight end position more, but not enough to make the schedule become a factor in deciding which tight end to draft. Another major reason tight ends are excluded from schedule considerations is because only about a third of the league uses the position with much regularity and success; and that means measuring what defenses are allowing tight ends cannot be accurate because it depends on how many times each defense faced a top 10 tight end.

But when the schedule is compared to what defenses allow to quarterbacks the past season, it is a very good tool. No matter how the quarterback scored his fantasy points, there is only one quarterback on every play and, while each will use a different mixture of receivers according to their offensive scheme, it's all about what each defense allowed that one guy who sticks his hands in the center's crotch every play. Passing is controlled by game situation, but when only one player is passing the ball it becomes reliable enough to consider.

When the schedule is compared to what defenses allow to running backs, it becomes a great tool. I have done the analysis for over

15 years now, and there is absolutely no position easier to predict than running back. There is no position as intimately affected by the schedule as running back. While the ease of schedule has only minor correlation with wide receivers and tight ends, and it will impact quarterbacks to a fair degree, all but the very best running backs will struggle to be better than what their schedule suggests.

ROLLING YOUR OWN

The Fantasy Ease of Schedule has been offered on The Huddle since 1997; but if you truly want to reach The Next Level, you should create your own, customized with your wisdom and knowledge to make it a powerful tool and help you draft better players— you know, the guys that are going to score the most fantasy points and not just the guys that get a trip to Hawaii for the Pro Bowl at the end of the season.

The first step in creating an ease of schedule is to determine the fantasy points allowed by each defense from the previous season for at least the two main positions of running back and quarterback. While I'll always carry receivers as well on The Huddle, there is less need to do it, as it is much less reliable than the quarterbacks and running backs. You can use the particular scoring results from your own league but you'll need access to the statistics allowed by each defense each week—not just what a team did offensively. This could entail copying weekly results to a spreadsheet and logging them not as the offensive team but what defense was allowing those yardage and points that week.

This will require some proficiency at working a spreadsheet, but it is a skill well worth having. Plus, when you are at your desk at your place of employment, it looks like you are legitimately doing work. You are of course, just not actually for your employer. Perception is everything in Corporate America.

SAMPLE AVERAGE POINTS ALLOWED TO RB'S

STL	23.6	CLE	20.1	MIN	17.7	SD	15.9
HOU	22.8	TEN	19.5	BAL	17.2	CIN	15.7
BUF	22.5	NO	19.2	MIA	17.2	PIT	15.5
SF	22.5	PHI	19.0	NE	16.8	JAX	15.0
OAK	22.1	ARI	18.9	KC	16.6	DEN	14.8
NYJ	22.0	WAS	18.8	TB	16.3	CHI	14.3
ATL	21.3	GB	18.3	DAL	16.1	CAR	14.3
DET	20.6	NYG	18.2	IND	16.1	SEA	13.6

Figure 18.1

What you will need to end up with is a listing of what each defense allowed to opposing quarterbacks and running backs on a weekly basis: fantasy points—not just yardage or touchdowns or whatever. There is enough similarity in scoring systems that it doesn't significantly affect the results no matter what you will likely use. Summing up what each defense allowed to the position and dividing by the number of games (16) will yield values similar to a sample from 2005 using a standard performance scoring (see figure 18.1).

Now this alone is worthy of use for making a schedule analysis since it objectively shows what each defense allowed to running backs for a weekly average over the course of 16 games from the previous season. However, it can be refined for an even more reliable result. There are a few realities about how numbers act when they are averaged that can conceal how they were accrued. First off, the NFL season typically starts out with the first two weeks being the highest-scoring of the season. The player performances are often surprising in those first two games because defenses have not prepared well enough or the offenses are not known well enough to defend against. While 2005 was an aberration, in most years the first two weeks will result in far more games that hit "the over" than those that fall below "the under."

Removing those first two games gives a better indication of what defenses from the past season were like. Removing the final game of the season should be done as well because so many teams are either resting players for the playoffs or trying out new players for off-season decision making that those weekly results are not accurate. After those three games have been removed there is one more adjustment to make last year's statistics be as revealing as possible: viewing the remaining fantasy points allowed between weeks three and 16 of the previous season, and then removing both the highest and lowest scores during the year. This helps to flatten out the peaks that were not indicative of what a defense typically allowed. To show the difference that comes from removing the first two weeks, the final week, and then culling out the highest and lowest scores, consider what the remaining 11 games calculated out to when using the same sample league (see Appendix, Table XV).

This yields the most accurate picture possible of what defenses were allowing to running backs the previous season without the effects of uncharacteristic games that happen at the first and last weeks of the year, nor skewing from the highest or lowest games allowed. Feel free to play around with including or excluding certain weeks—there are dozens of ways to make up a listing. After almost two decades of this sort of analysis, I have settled on the previously described method as the best—I have tried just about all the others and keep coming back to this method as the most sound.

The natural question is: How reliable are these numbers in reality? Defenses do change from year to year, to be sure, but within any given season, the average shift in ranking will be about five spots per team. Half will exceed that mark and half will fall below it. About one in four teams will change more than 10 ranking positions. This is why such analysis is only a guideline. However, for those teams that do change dramatically from one year to the next the reasons are usually outside the realm of predictability. Every year there will be at least four or five NFL teams that are so racked by injuries that they have a major impact on their ranking. And a similar amount will rise dramatically either by the addition of particular players (which can be accounted for) or because their season is exceptionally good and favorably impacts their defense (which can be due to their schedule). This is a tool to be used as a guideline and can certainly be altered by your own judgment calls.

Once you have that ordered ranking of what each team defense has allowed the previous season, you can apply it to the upcoming season in one of two ways. If you are in a total points league, it is as simple as replacing each weekly opponent with their fantasy points allowed, on a grid. That can reveal valuable information (see figure 18.2).

In total points leagues, it's obvious in this sample that the Falcons would have the toughest schedule both during the regular fantasy season and the playoffs as well. The Cardinals have the best schedule during the regular season (weeks one to 13) and yet the Bills have an excellent schedule during the playoffs in this sample. This is all information that can be used in your decision-making process.

More commonly fantasy leagues use head-to-head games and so the overall points matter far less than how they are acquired. It's great to have two weeks with astronomic scores but if they are followed by six or eight bad match-ups, there could be better schedules to chase than one with good overall points but not many easier games. Using the ranked array of what each team allowed

COMPARING EACH WEEK AGAINST FANTASY POINTS ALLOWED BY THAT OPPONENT

Week	1	2	3	4	5	6	7	8	9	10	11	12	13	14	15	16	Overall Points	Weeks 1–13	Weeks 14–16
ARI	21	16	25	22	16	15	20	20	bye	17	22	17	25	14	15	21	286	236	50
ATL	13	17	14	18	bye	19	15	17	21	18	16	15	20	17	17	13	250	203	47
BAL	17	20	18	16	16	13	bye	18	17	20	22	16	17	16	18	17	261	210	51
BUF	16	17	22	17	14	21	16	bye	20	16	22	15	18	22	24	20	280	214	66
CAR	22	17	17	18	18	16	16	17	bye	17	25	20	19	19	16	22	279	222	57

Figure 18.2

to runners from the previous season, you can make head-to-head scheduling easier by considering each match-up against a top 10 defense (allowing the least points) as a bad game with a value of 1. Take the worst 10 teams in the listing (allowing the most points) and award a point for each match-up with them. For those middle 12 teams, do not award any points. Then it is simply a counting of "good" games versus "bad" games to determine which teams face the easiest and hardest schedules.

Using the 10 best and worst defenses respects the fact that defenses change about five spots on average per year. Those middle teams act as a buffer between the best and worst match-ups suggested by what defenses actually did the previous season. As with the total points example above, you can slice and dice the numbers according to any grouping of weeks that you want. And here is where we can recall a previous rule:

Rule 6

There is nothing as important as having a genuine feel for the game.

This is your ease of schedule, and you can certainly adjust the results by considering particular match-ups as good or bad despite the statistics not showing that. If there is a reason that you believe a defense will perform much better in the current year than the previous season, then consider the match-up as bad. If you see peril on the horizon and think the season will prove to be a major downer for a defense, then consider the match-up as good. It's your schedule—make it reflect your thoughts.

MINING THE WAIVER WIRE

"If you scratch the surface and find the worm, the early bird gets nothing . . ."

THERE IS NO FANTASY TEAM OWNER who enters the season thinking that they will rely on the waiver wire to create their team. After all, depending on the league size, the annual draft just supposedly scooped up the best 150 to 300 players in the NFL. What could possibly be left? The reality is not a lot . . . but definitely enough. While we all go through various levels of preparation before we draft, it is delightfully impossible to grab every single fantasy-relevant player, if only because team dynamics change and players get injured. The waiver wire is the one place that everyone has equal access to in order to get replacement players (aka "bury your dead").

If there is one characteristic that defines all great fantasy owners, it is that they constantly churn the lowest part of their roster. They are looking not only for the next surprise superstar but also just for any player that could be 1 percent better than what they have. Some leagues have massive trading but most leagues have only a few trades per year. Some leagues never have trades or are even not allowed to have them. The waiver wire is that mini-draft that occurs each week of the season and is possibly the only way to better your team—every week, if possible.

Rule 23

Never, ever be satisfied with your roster. Churn for improvement.

The quality and depth found on the waiver wire is in direct proportion to how many teams are in the league and how many players there are already on rosters, as well as some homage paid to the realities of certain positions. Each league will be different from another because it will have a unique set of players either already on rosters or still available on the waiver wire. While that may prevent highly league-specific information and advice from being included here, there are enough generalities to merit a discussion of how The Next Level uses the waiver wire.

For some basis in reality, I reviewed a five-year sample for players who were not drafted in the average league (12 teams, 18-man rosters) and will include the results of those merely as a sample of the sort of players who have most often come from the waiver wire. Obviously smaller leagues and smaller rosters would have more and better players, while bigger leagues would have even fewer. The players listed are a decent though not all-inclusive sample. Their rankings stem from the most common performance league scoring of $\frac{1}{10}$ point per yard rushed or received; $\frac{1}{20}$ point per yard passed; six-point touchdowns other than passing, which count three points; and all two-point conversion participants getting two points. The rankings shown are for that position during that year. Chances are pretty good the players were not taken in your leagues as well.

UNDRAFTED OR RELEASED QUARTERBACKS

Since most leagues only start one quarterback, that means that typically about 24 or so are drafted (two per team). That suggests that there are still starters left on the waiver wire in most leagues as well as almost all backup quarterbacks. What sort of quarterbacks did the waiver wire produce over a five-year span? The results from one expert league (Site Owners Football Association—SOFA) over a five-year period (see figure 19.1) give a good indication of what free agents were available in those seasons. Chances are that your league had at least these, if not many more.

Only twice in a five-year span did the waiver wire actually produce a player who ended up worth starting in an average 12-team league, and even then they barely ranked high enough to merit starting. Sure, Kurt Warner set the bar ridiculously high on what an unknown quarterback can do but that highly unusual season is not worth remembering.

This is not to say that the waiver wire is not important for quarterbacks, but the reality is that you are not likely to find a big-time player on it. If you need a quarterback, you'll likely be better off arranging a trade, since any worthy quarterback is most likely going to be on another team if it is early in the season. Reviewing the same five-year period, the top 10 quarterbacks each season (measured by points per game) did not typically miss much time either, so grabbing their backup on the hope they would stumble rarely paid off. The one exception here is for backup quarterbacks in systems that are known to throw often and well. Historically, backup quarterbacks from St. Louis, Arizona, and Minnesota have fared very well in brief showings. If there is a backup worth grabbing, it is from a high-powered passing team with the starter missing games.

The position almost never produces fantasy-relevant players who are in their first year or two other than those pass-happy offenses (typically with substandard defenses). Just because a quarterback is injured is no reason to assume that his backup is going to

EXPERT SOFA LEAGUE WAIVER WIRE QUARTERBACKS— 5-YEAR SAMPLE

Fantasy Rank	Year	Player	Pts	Fantasy Rank	Year	Player	Pts
10	2001	Kordell Stewart	268	18	2005	Gus Frerotte	182
11	2004	Drew Brees	250	19	2001	Chris Weinke	216
13	2005	Mark Brunell	217	21	2001	Jon Kitna	202
14	2002	Chad Pennington	231	21	2002	Tommy Maddox	201
14	2003	Quincy Carter	223	21	2004	Ben Roethlisberger	182
15	2003	Jake Delhomme	204	22	2003	Jeff Blake	161
16	2002	Jon Kitna	228	23	2001	Tom Brady	193
16	2004	Vinny Testaverde	215	23	2004	Brian Griese	178
18	2002	Matt Hasselbeck	218	24	2002	David Carr	189
18	2003	Byron Leftwich	183	24	2005	Trent Dilfer	141

Figure 19.1

THE REGULAR SEASON AND BEYOND

be a great waiver wire pick. Much more often than not, his replacement is a significant step down. Since there are usually other starting quarterbacks on the waiver wire with more of a track record, they usually make better choices. Regardless—keep your expectations fairly low.

UNDRAFTED OR RELEASED RUNNING BACKS

Ah yes, this is the reason the waiver wire exists—at least for most people. If you are looking for the one area to constantly churn trying to find a better player (or at least keep them from other teams in your league), it is definitely running back. Despite the frenzied run on the position in most leagues during the draft, we all know that some gems have been pulled from the waiver wire and, at times, they are true difference-makers (see figure 19.2).

Considering that each league typically starts two running backs and some even allow three, there have been several nice finds on the waiver wire. Over the five-year sample, four of the five years had undrafted running backs end up as being starting fantasy backs *over the course of a full season*. That there would be any seems almost unthinkable given how much interest there is in the position during drafts. Where did those top players come from?

- **Injured Starters** Dominic Rhodes, Marcel Shipp, Nick Goings, and Maurice Smith were merely on the sideline when the starter was injured early in the season and then delivered like they were drafted in the first few rounds that summer. This is especially relevant for the running back position: See chapter 8 for an in-depth discussion. In 2006, Ladell Betts shined once Clinton Portis went down as well.

EXPERT SOFA LEAGUE WAIVER WIRE RUNNING BACKS— 5-YEAR SAMPLE

Fantasy Rank	Year	Player	Pts	Fantasy Rank	Year	Player	Pts
10	2001	Dominic Rhodes	182	34	2004	Chester Taylor	97
13	2004	Reuben Droughns	192	35	2004	Sammy Morris	96
14	2003	Domanick Davis	179	35	2005	Samkon Gado	118
19	2003	Rudi Johnson	159	38	2002	Kevin Faulk	94
21	2002	Marcel Shipp	167	38	2004	Antowain Smith	87
22	2004	Nick Goings	156	38	2005	Marion Barber	108
24	2001	Maurice Smith	126	39	2001	Bob Christian	81
29	2002	Moe Williams	122	39	2002	James Mungro	85
30	2004	Derrick Blaylock	127	40	2005	Tony Fisher	101
33	2003	Richie Anderson	103	41	2003	Rock Cartwright	75

Figure 19.2

THE REGULAR SEASON AND BEYOND

- **Depth Chart Surprises** When everyone was trying to guess which Denver back to grab in the summer of 2004, no one thought to look at the second-string fullback. Denver has long been a haven of surprise studs and Reuben Droughns was likely the biggest of them all. Similarly, Domanick Davis was injured during his first training camp and no one had seen him play. He went undrafted in many leagues but ended up winning the starting job in 2003 and started to excel by week six.

- **Developing Situations** Rudi Johnson played behind Corey Dillon in 2003 when Dillon was injured and occasionally challenged to get to the stadium on time. Johnson has never looked back. While injury obviously changes the depth charts, attitude and poor play by the starter can as well.

What figure 19.2 does not reflect are the many running backs who may only get a limited number of starts in a season, but for those games, they have definite fantasy value that you can either use or at least deny to another team that may need it worse than you do. There is no position to churn like running backs. At the first sign a starter appears to be dinged up, grab the second guy.

UNDRAFTED OR RELEASED TIGHT ENDS

The chance that you can find a great tight end on the waiver wire is almost nil unless some other team has dumped a drafted player. Consider that there are rarely more than a dozen in the position with fantasy relevance (which itself may be generous) and with often double that drafted, not too many fall through the cracks. Still, it does happen to a small degree (see figure 19.3).

EXPERT SOFA LEAGUE WAIVER WIRE TIGHT ENDS— 5-YEAR SAMPLE

Fantasy Rank	Year	Player	Pts	Fantasy Rank	Year	Player	Pts
4	2003	Boo Williams	68	8	2001	David Sloan	78
7	2002	Billy Miller	73	13	2004	Chris Cooley	63
7	2003	Itula Mili	66	14	2001	Anthony Becht	56
7	2004	Jermaine Wiggins	87	14	2004	Jeb Putzier	63
8	2004	Eric Johnson	86	15	2001	Dwayne Carswell	52

Figure 19.3

While there have been top 10 tight ends showing up on the waiver wire after being missed in the draft, the reality is that none of these came from recent years. Prior to 2004, tight end scoring was mostly the top three, and the rest really had little difference. Now that there are eight to 10 very good tight ends each season, the waiver wire wonders are all but gone. Other than needing to fill a bye week, the waiver wire for tight ends is sparse enough that anyone you get will not provide any difference-making points. It requires an elite tight end in an offense designed to use him for there to be any reliable consistency and production worth tracking.

UNDRAFTED OR RELEASED WIDE RECEIVERS

This position is almost always used in greater number than any other in fantasy leagues. Most will use three of them and occasionally even four starters per week (considering a flex position). They are also among the toughest of NFL players to forecast each season. This results in several starters coming out of the undrafted pool —and over a period of time, some downright great players for that year. Anquan Boldin may go down in fantasy history as the best undrafted wide receiver ever since the rookie was overlooked in most leagues in 2003. That's okay—even the Arizona scouts were surprised, since the Cardinals grabbed Bryant Johnson in the first round and waited until the second to get Boldin.

After Boldin, the only other player that managed a WR1 sort of season after being undrafted in most leagues was Brandon Stokley, who turned the #3 position in Indianapolis into more than what two thirds of the rest of NFL teams had for a #1 wideout. Of course that was followed by a typical year by Stokley, so chalk that one up to a delightful find in 2004 but nothing to reliably expect.

As we saw back in the analyzing wide receivers chapter (9), many of the players in figure 19.4 were future studs who were in their second year or even their third with minimal track record to suggest that a breakout season was in store. But it obviously happens. Figure that each team uses at least two wideouts with some regularity (flanker and split end). That means there are 64 starters in the NFL, which is more than enough to give six to each fantasy team in a league of 10. And that doesn't count the large number of situations that will develop as the season progresses or the incidence of injury that promotes wideouts into greater playing time.

Wide receivers are definitely worth tracking on the waiver wire, which should be reviewed every week not only for players that were undrafted but, equally important, for players that have been released by other teams because of a slow start or a lack of roster room and needs in other areas. What to look for?

EXPERT SOFA LEAGUE WAIVER WIRE WIDEOUTS— 5-YEAR SAMPLE

Fantasy Rank	Year	Player	Pts	Fantasy Rank	Year	Player	Pts
4	2003	Anquan Boldin	182	32	2004	David Patten	115
11	2004	Brandon Stokley	161	33	2002	Steve Smith	111
15	2001	Marty Booker	151	35	2003	Bobby Engram	92
15	2003	Steve Smith	148	36	2004	Keary Colbert	101
17	2002	Chad Johnson	142	38	2004	Ronald Curry	99
20	2002	Quincy Morgan	137	39	2001	Raghib Ismail	92
22	2003	Justin McCareins	118	39	2003	Bobby Shaw	90
30	2001	Hines Ward	121	40	2005	Ernest Wilford	139
31	2002	Dennis Northcutt	113	42	2003	David Givens	83
31	2004	T. J. Houshmandzadeh	120	42	2002	Tai Streets	100

Figure 19.4

- **Developing Situations** Easily the most common source for waiver wire gems, no position goes through the transition that wide receivers do each season. This has to do with receiver talent more than anything, which typically indicates that they are young and getting better. It is very rare for a wideout more than four or five seasons in the NFL to suddenly develop into being a very good player. They just won't get the chance more than anything.

- **Demise of the Rushing Game** When a team experiences a reduction in their rushing game either because of a running back injury or a soft defense that forces a team to throw, then all the receivers on that team will become more valuable from the increase in sheer volume of passes.

- **Injury to Starters** While this does give everyone a bump up on the depth chart, unless it is a relatively young receiver with developing talent, not much will likely happen other than a small increase due to more passes. Keep in mind—a receiver may get more passes but does that actually make him fantasy-relevant in your league?

Next to running backs, the waiver wire is most productive for wide receivers, but there is a distinct difference between what you need to consider. Running backs mostly need opportunity that was unforeseen in fantasy drafts whereas wide receivers need to show that their talent level is increasing beyond expectations. While all positions will have waiver wire needs because of injuries and bye weeks, the running backs and wideouts are the two to track for unexpected opportunity or situation. Grab your quarterbacks and tight ends if you need them but keep expectations low. Track those tailbacks and wideouts because the dynamics of the season will make your waiver wire pay off in those positions.

UNDRAFTED OR RELEASED PLACEKICKERS

As was shown in the analyzing placekickers chapter, there is precious little difference between most kickers, and many if not most fantasy team owners rely on the waiver wire to at least cover bye weeks if not pick up a new kicker to start. So long as you have selected a kicker as suggested in Chapter 11, in most cases you should hang on to him even if he is no longer your starter. Many kickers come around later in the year.

Remember—kickers are merely an expression of the effectiveness of an offense. Kickers who are scoring well tend to continue to score well. Unless your kickers are just far below average or you see a kicker on the waiver wire who has put together several consecutive good games, it is wise to not spend your waiver wire picks chasing down a kicker. If an offense suddenly "has the wheels fall off" during the season thanks to injuries and team dynamics, then don't wait for your kicker to prove that the offense is going downhill.

The waiver wire produces many good players each season though very rarely a true star. Instead, it is there to help you improve your team even if only by 1 percent. It takes wisdom and reason to decide when to release one player and acquire another and those at The Next Level know how to work that. All that you do in the preseason should prepare you for recognizing a good acquisition, in particular when you go through the process of projecting player performance based on past statistics—particularly the weekly ones.

When you mine the waiver wire, you are just looking for value. It doesn't matter if that player you get is one that you never use. You need that option in case of injury, and in the NFL—you just never exactly know what is going to happen. If a player is going to exceed expectations, it makes more sense for him to benefit you, not someone else in your league.

PREPARING FOR THE PLAYOFFS

"Play for the trophy, the thrill of competition, the sweet taste of victory—and the chance to ridicule all your friends."

LITTLE IS SWEETER THAN WINNING your fantasy league championship. Sure, you probably get some hardware in the way of a trophy. You might even get "the league check" to cash. But above all, you get the satisfaction of knowing that you navigated a 16-week minefield better than anyone else in your league and you have a full year to constantly remind your league mates of the admirable feat. You are the king, champion, victor, the man, top dog, numero uno . . . there are many more terms but I usually get "Shut up, already" before I can exhaust the list.

At least one of the reasons that we all play fantasy football is to win the league championship, and likely it is the primary goal in the same way that you work to earn a living and not just for a chance to wear khaki pants and surf the Net away from home. The ring is the thing, and getting to the playoffs is all that matters—right?

In a sense of priority—sure, it is the first goal. But just getting there is not the end game. Winning the championship is. When you draft your team in the summer, your aim is to assemble the best possible team you can so that you win more games than anyone. But when the season reaches the midpoint and your team is still in contention, what can you do to increase your chances in your fantasy postseason? There are three main considerations you must address before most of the league stops playing and starts watching your ascension to the throne.

THE SCHEDULE, THE SCHEDULE, THE SCHEDULE

When you drafted your team, hopefully you took into account the overall schedule that each player was to face that year, since it is a significant factor for every player once you get past the fantasy studs. If you have more than two studs on your team, consider yourself a very shrewd, crafty team owner (though everyone else will chalk it up to dumb luck). Giving some consideration to the schedule, when you initially draft players it makes sense to acquire those with the softest match-ups while avoiding any players that have a brutal stretch to end their season. Yes, you do have to get there for it to matter but you also want to avoid getting waxed once you get there. No one much remembers who ended up in second place and they certainly have no idea who came in fourth.

If you are playing in a contest that uses one week as the lone determination if your team will advance in the playoffs, you better know exactly what the match-ups are before you ever draft a player. That doesn't necessarily mean to avoid drafting a running back who will spend the first two weeks of the playoffs going against the two best rush defenses in the NFL. It does mean you do not necessarily have to still own him by the time you get there.

During the summer when you are reviewing the players you may draft, you absolutely should take a gander at who he will be facing in those final weeks. Only in the extreme cases of the worst schedules should it make you want to avoid a player. And even the best schedule won't matter that much for an average player unless you can feel confident that his match-ups will still look just as easy (or formidable) in week 10 as they did back in August. But every year there are players who start hot and then fade and often that is related to the change in their schedule strength. Draft those players if it makes sense, but be prepared to "sell high" on them and get someone else who appears an equivalent but who has a kinder schedule when you need it most.

This illustrates a very important fact. In the summer, you are basing your perceptions about the schedule from past statistics allowed by the defense and factoring in whatever change in team dynamics that may affect them this year. After the first month of the season is completed, you will have far better insight into what defenses will be like that season. At The Huddle, we reevaluate the schedule every four games just to monitor what defenses are actually like for the season. The main reason—the playoffs. You need to know which teams will enjoy a relative cakewalk and which teams get the short end of the ease of schedule stick.

The reality is that while you acquired players for their overall value, most playoffs are about head-to-head match-ups where you must outscore your weekly opponent or you go home. The regular season is about the overall performance of your team compared to all others in the league. The playoffs are single-game events where you must play better than your one opponent, even if he has the second highest score in the league that week. That means the defensive match-ups are critical. Taking the less defended road really can make all the difference.

Rule 24

Defensive match-ups are critical in the playoffs.

Most leagues have rules where trades cannot occur once the playoffs begin, so if you realize that one of your average players seems likely to get crushed in week 14, you had better at least investigate the chance of trading him away for a better option. Where to look? How about those teams in your leagues that are on the periphery of making the playoffs and must win now or risk missing the postseason? Provided you are in a comfortable situation with making the playoffs, it is perfectly acceptable to swap players with another team to give him the best match-ups now in exchange for your new player having a better time in the playoffs. You must know your players and schedule before taking that route but it can be rather effective. It may even bring calls of unfairness by other teams that know what you are doing and do not like being helpless to stop it.

Living with the NFL schedule should be a season-long obsession since it is a long-term predictive tool in addition to being important the week when you figure out your starting lineup. While you may not usually consider the schedule when drafting defenses and kickers (and no one would really blame you), it does come into play in those playoff weeks. While it is better to have the kicker who kicked two field goals in a 32–6 loss than it is to use a kicker who only had five extra points in a 35–3 blowout, that cannot be reasonably forecast. The waiver wire can often produce better options for you with kickers and defenses for those critical weeks at the end of the season—take a look at what you have and what is available.

BACKUPS MAY BE YOUR ONLY SURE STARTERS

Figure your roster is likely comprised of a quarterback you always start and some average player as a backup. You are probably fairly set at running backs and most of your starting decisions each week fall to your wide receiver corps. Let it ride or consider further mining of the waiver wire or trades to shore up your team? While churning the lowest part of your roster is a necessary activity during the season, realize that by the end of the year there are far fewer developing situations to take advantage of. The flops have already flopped by midseason, for the most part, and the "I did not see that coming" studs have already taken their starting roles. Where a change in player value comes will most likely be from injuries to starters that yield new opportunity to backups. And what if that injured player was yours?

3-YEAR SAMPLE— RB GAMES MISSED AFTER A HEALTHY WEEK 13

		Week 14	Week 15	Week 16	Week 17
2005	Chris Brown			X	X
2005	Domanick Davis		X	X	X
2005	LaMont Jordan			X	X
2005	Brian Westbrook	X	X	X	X
2004	Chris Brown		X	X	X
2004	Clinton Portis			X	X
2004	Fred Taylor			X	X
2004	Brian Westbrook			X	X
2003	Clinton Portis			X	X

Figure 20.1

I lost a championship in 2002 because in week 15 I had my three highest-scoring players fall to injury—Terrell Owens, Priest Holmes, and Steve McNair. While I pretend to diminish the pain of that championship loss by referring to it as the "Asterisk Bowl," the reality was that I had not accommodated the worst-case scenario as well as I should have. One year in the World Championship of Fantasy Football (WCOFF), I had all three of my quarterbacks become injured in one week. Another league member was nice enough to use all his remaining free agency money to buy up the four best remaining quarterbacks on the waiver wire just to leave me virtually nothing. Injuries can happen any week and no doubt you too have felt this pinch if you have played long enough.

This falls back to the question you should have asked your-self during your draft—should I back up this player? For your stud players the answer is almost always "yes." Absolutely for a stud super back and, when you near the playoffs, you should even con-sider backing up quarterbacks. Whether you still have access to the waiver wire that late in the year or not, getting the backup for your stars means that you can be sure you will have someone to start if the worst-case scenario happens. Think about it—your current backup may be an NFL starter in the league but he can be injured in the same week as your starter. Trust me—it can happen. Not so for your starter's backup, who is safely clutching a clipboard.

THE DREADED RESTING-FOR-THE-PLAYOFFS

The final consideration that is hard to gauge but should be weighed is the chance that your stud players are on an NFL team that is coasting toward the postseason and may decide to rest them up as early as week 15 or week 16 (see figure 20.2). It is a nightmarish situation, usually because so often they will play but only in a lim-ited role, and you will have to decide how limited it will be when you make your starting decisions. If only in this one way, be glad there is more parity in the league now because there are more teams fighting for a playoff spot through the final games of the regular season.

Unfortunately, in those situations, you will need to monitor your roster for what it can provide in those final weeks. In some years (like 2003) this is not a problem. In other seasons, there will usually be a couple of quarterbacks or running backs that you can-not rely on in week 17. It all depends on what the divisional records are later in the year. In 2005, Peyton Manning had only a cameo in week 16 before resting in week 17—bad timing for his fantasy owners.

PLAYERS EITHER RESTED OR USED SPARINGLY IN WEEK 17

	2001	2002	2003	2004	2005
Top 12 Quarterbacks	1	1	0	2	4
Top 24 Running Backs	2	0	0	5	3

Figure 20.2

The safest of all moves is to enter the playoffs with your best starting quarterback, another starter from a different team, and the backup for your best quarterback. That way you can either cover an injury or a rest-for-the-playoffs with your #2 quarterback or still have the option of turning to your star's backup player. The problem with those players who are rested is that often they will play a cameo role and will water down what even their backup can do, since they will not play a full game.

This could mean hanging on to your current players, knowing that you may need to rely on them because there is no certainty how much the backup of your stud will play. He could become the full-game starter and have a big week or he could watch the stud play the first half and then go in and finish the game with other backup players who will not move the ball as well as the normal starters.

When your season is going well and you are confident that a postseason berth is in store for you, make sure you are aware of the schedule for each of your players, back up the ones that you cannot afford to lose, and make preparations in case your stars get the hated time off at the end of the year. The only surprise you want in the playoffs is just how over-the-top your trophy acceptance speech will be.

WHY FANTASY FOOTBALL IS *GOOD* FOR THE WORKPLACE 21

"Fantasy football owners cost employers as much as $1.1 billion a week in lost productivity."

(Reuters, "Fantasy Football Sacks Real Work Production," August 16, 2006)

THAT'S THE MOST POPULAR NUMBER being bandied about the world of television, newspapers, magazines, and the Internet about how much money companies are losing due to productivity drops attributed to fantasy football. It is the sort of number that is drawn from the candy bowl of meaningless statistics at a board of directors meeting and used to alert everyone of the impending doom to year end bonuses. I believe the same number was initially used to describe the devastating corporate impact of the solitaire game that comes with the Windows operating system.

First off—that number was created by a study done for a national job placement firm and was derived by taking a supposed universe of 37 million fantasy footballers (about double the number typically used) against a meaningless national average wage and then grabbing out of the air a subjective 50 minutes per week they spent on their teams instead of working. They multiplied this on a very big calculator and now the media and boardrooms are hanging decisions on a fabricated fact that businesses are losing $1.1 billion per week that evidently they would have gained without fantasy football in the workplace. And people get paid to come up with numbers like that—seriously.

Figuring that the average person takes about an hour lunch each day would therefore suggest that U.S. companies are losing

$5 billion weekly because employees are eating leftover meat loaf at their desk or running down to the closest sandwich shop. Hey look—I can do this too!

But such a number is created and then lands into an article that your boss reads. And then he has an employee come into his office. Maybe it is some lady in trouble for surfing celebrity Web sites all day. Maybe it is a guy who is chronically late to work because he uses his evening hours to ignite his fledgling career as a rock star. Whoever it is, rather than take responsibility for what they have done, they do the natural thing—they throw you and your league mates under the proverbial bus.

"Yeah, well, those guys on the second floor do NOTHING all day but talk about fantasy football."

"Oh really . . . ?"

It can happen a thousand different ways but the end result is usually the same—a corporate crackdown on the evils of fantasy football, which is supported by—look at this! $1.1 billion per week lost by companies! Suddenly the ranking of company evils tucks fantasy football between embezzlement and parking in the CEO's reserved spot (actually, reverse those two). It's even much, much worse than taking home company pencils, which is another pointless stat that humorless statisticians with no real-world experience use to justify their jobs.

Next thing you know, that momentary jaunt to TheHuddle .com or ESPN suddenly returns a screen that says "Page Blocked," aka "Not today, slacker." Suddenly there are corporate brownshirts on the prowl listening for any whispered conversation that contains "quarterback," "touchdown," or "the bastard went out on the one-yard line." Corporate e-mail filters begin to search for words like "Roethlisberger" or "sleeper." You are an outcast now. You must stamp your forehead with "FF" and once again start climbing up the corporate caste system. Work shirker! Waster of company profits! All that is left is for Bill Lumbergh from the movie *Office Space* to show up at your cubicle.

"Ahh, I'm going to have to go ahead and ask you to come in on Sunday too . . ."

Such is the reality at some workplaces. Most moderately tolerate it if they have not read "the article" yet. Too few look the other way as long as the work they are paying you for is getting done. But—I am here to make one claim. Businesses should not prohibit it. They should embrace it and realize that it makes for better employees.

Before we proceed there is one significant caveat. It doesn't matter if it is fantasy football, collecting comic books, or bass fishing. If an employee has an obsession that impacts the quality and quantity of work that he or she does, it is fair enough for any business to prohibit it from the workplace. You are not compensated with a salary just for sitting in a particular chair the required amount of time each day, at least not in the private sector. You are employed to perform an agreed level of work for which the company will pay you. Do your work to an acceptable level—they have to pay you. If your work is not acceptable, they can get rid of you or travel other unsavory paths. As a manager for many years in a large corporation, I was amazed how those facts escaped so many employees. But the bottom line—if you do your work, then fantasy sports are a benefit to the workplace.

FANTASY FOOTBALL—THE KEY TO INCREASING COMPANY PROFITS

It is in the interest of every company to employ people who will create the products or services desired and by that earn a profit for their employer. The better all employees do together, the better the company will do. Introducing, or at least allowing, fantasy football in the workplace not only makes for a happier employee, it increases the skills and abilities that mark a valuable worker.

Unlike other interests and hobbies that make their way into the work environment, fantasy football provides a training course or at least a refresher in the traits of a successful organization. By taking leadership of their own "team" during the course of the NFL season, they will step through the checklist of a model employee.

Let's pretend that you and I are employees of SuperBigCorp who have been called into a conference room with 10 other co-workers. A pert young lady wearing dark-rimmed glasses and some insanely poofy scarf around her neck waits for everyone to be seated. She checks off some items on her clipboard and then sets it on the table while she informs you that the company has developed a new employee-improvement program that offers workers the chance to create a fantasy football league.

". . . and at the conclusion of the four-month period that coincides with the NFL season, we will evaluate each person in the league to determine if they have learned and exhibited the desired characteristics, skills, and abilities necessary for success."

She starts pointing at a list of words on the white board and explaining their meaning.

Teamwork   You are tasked with assembling this group as a league of fantasy team owners. You must determine who will be the league manager by a popular vote and that this "commissioner" will be entrusted with maintaining the health of the league and ensuring that all rules are adhered to in addition to organizing any and all team activities to include a draft and an awards ceremony for the winner. You must all come together to create an agreed upon set of league rules that all must follow and the group must devise a scoring system that is viewed as fair to all teams. You must end with a clear winner of the league in an agreed upon fashion. You must all work together as a team.

Multitasking   Through the entirety of the four months, you must ensure that your work here never suffers and that this fantasy league does not impact your ability to do your job at SuperBigCorp.

You must make the decisions regarding when you will work on this league and then adopt it seamlessly into your work flow. You must perform task prioritizing each week for the next four months, never failing to give your fantasy team the needed attention while doing so only after you have ensured that your needed SuperBigCorp work will be completed as required.

Improvement-Oriented You will not be allowed to merely field a fantasy team and then ride it through the season. You must continually analyze your roster and starting lineup for improvement by way of a waiver wire or by trading as sanctioned by the league. You must improve your team with every opportunity that you find. An improvement of just 1 percent in your team can result in winning more games and an eventual championship. Always strive for improvement.

Adaptability Your team may suffer injuries or other dynamics that were unforeseen when originally created. You must show the ability to adapt to the new situation and make the best of it. You cannot merely accept a setback and do nothing about it. You must respond to change in a positive, reasonable manner with an eye for at least maintaining your status quo if not improving it. You must adapt.

Sound Judgment You must exhibit sound judgment when creating and maintaining your team. Failure to show proper judgment will impede your ability to field an optimal team. In the event that your judgment fails on a player or a strategic move, you must show that you have learned from the mistake and incorporate that into your future ability to judge people, situations, and potential outcomes. You must exhibit an ever increasing ability to make sound judgments based upon what you have learned and done.

Ethics During the course of your season, you may encounter situations where you have privileged information that others do not have. You must not act unethically in trying to induce others to take action based on flawed information or beliefs. You will be judged on how you treated the members of this league. If you act outside of the agreed upon rules, you can be subject to sanctions or even dismissal from the league. You must act ethically in all that you do.

Competition   You must understand that while you will show ethical behavior you must work together as a team, you are in competition with each other. Your success will be measured not on your potential and not on your relationship with the commissioner. It will be tallied from the metrics of wins and losses of your team over the course of the season. You must compete each week and the management of your team must be in the interest of fielding the most competitive squad possible.

Security and Safety   You must demonstrate your concern about the security of your roster and the safety of your team in its entirety—not just one or two players. You must determine when you should acquire backups for your best players to ensure that you will continue to field an optimal team even in the event of misfortunes happening to your players. You must plan for contingencies even if they do not occur. You must also ensure the proper security for your team so that no one else is able to harm it. This means securing any passwords and making sure that only approved personnel have access to your team. You must demonstrate risk management for your team.

Recognition   Both as a league and as individual team owners, you must recognize other team owners for accomplishments including but not limited to winning the eventual championship. You must make the reward for winning worthwhile and a desired goal of every team member. At the awards ceremony, you must honor your league champion and publicize any other notable accomplishments by other team owners.

Through the process of creating and maintaining your fantasy team while demonstrating the above listed abilities, it is also expected that you will make personal improvement to a number of skills that should be a part of your normal work here at SuperBigCorp. These include but are not limited to:

Analytic Aptitude   You must show an increasing skill at analysis, where you can analyze the statistics generated by the NFL both this season and from previous years. You will understand what happened in the past and determine how that applies to your players—both currently owned and potentially acquired. You may use numerical modeling but must also show the ability to apply sound judgment based on nonnumerical events and conditions. Your team's future depends upon your ability to analyze the past and present.

Communication   Through the course of the season, you must devise the most effective and efficient manners of communication between team members and the league as a whole. You must ensure that all team owners remain completely informed of all league issues and situations and you must cultivate interpersonal relationships with other team owners to enact trades of players or assist each other with necessary tasks. You are expected to remain in communication during the four months with a dialogue that you all find enjoyable and entertaining if not informative as well. You must remain in communication with each other. You are not allowed to merely run a team in silence by yourself without any interaction with other team owners.

Decision Making and Problem Solving   These skills will be challenged on a continual basis. You must determine who the best players are to build an optimal team when it is your turn to draft. You must also respond to any problems that happen during the course of the season with reasoned and proactive decision making. While you are encouraged to consider the advice and information of others, it is you who must turn that into an action that affects only your team. You are responsible for the results of your team—no one else is. Your ability to make decisions and resolve problems will be critical to your team's success.

Forecasting   Managing a fantasy team is not about collecting players that have been good in the past, it is about acquiring them for their future value from which you will either profit or fail. You must exhibit the ability to turn past results and current dynamics into a reasonable and reliable view of the future from which you can make the proper decisions. This will entail the use of analysis, communication, information gathering, and some mathematical skills. You must determine a numerical expression of each player's future value and apply sound judgment to each regarding their reliability, opportunity, risk, and upside for the coming season.

Computer Skills   It is imperative that you are able to effectively use a computer during the management of your team. Your league must exist only in an electronic format and you must show an ability to interact with the league system in order to view your team, submit weekly lineups, conduct free agent transactions, and communicate with other members of your league. Additionally, it is encouraged that you learn either database or spreadsheet skills in order to perform your player analysis and create your projected statistics for each player. You must also be able to efficiently and effectively use the Internet for gaining knowledge that will be used in your analysis and decision-making processes.

You will be evaluated at the end of the season based on the performance of your team, which will be an expression of how well you used those skills and abilities. This cannot impact your normal work here at SuperBigCorp. Are you interested in joining the SuperBigCorp Fantasy Football League?

This is about the time that I would jump up and say "Well hell yeah!" (Author's note—I never was a great fit in the corporate world.) The question is: Would such a program create a better employee? *It had better, since each of the above skills and abilities comes directly from an employee evaluation form.* Collecting comic books or bass fishing may bring great value into many people's lives, but do they create a more skilled, capable employee? Fantasy football does. Name any other hobby that can have such a positive impact on the skills and abilities that employers want in their employees. Bet you can't.

Fantasy football is like a crash course in business that touches on almost every area of work that is desirable to employers. It plays out like a course in an MBA program with even more measurable results.

Here's the kicker—people enjoy playing fantasy football. It brings them together in a fun, competitive situation that only lasts about four months of the year. A pervasive problem in our country is the inability of companies to retain their best employees and make continued use of their skill sets. And so they want to squash the one activity that brings them together, gives them pleasure and entertainment, and reinforces every skill and ability that the company desires them to have? Curious, eh?

But hey, someone, somewhere, pulled the figure $1.1 billion out of the corporate ether and now hundreds if not thousands of people are playing solitaire at lunch instead of logging on to my or any other fantasy football Web site. I'm not bitter, just a bit perplexed. Oh yes, and you can be damn sure that I'll be keeping this pencil too . . .

THE FUTURE OF FANTASY FOOTBALL

(Captain Willard stares at the severed heads adorning Colonel Kurtz's headquarters)

Photo Journalist: *The heads. You're looking at the heads. Sometimes he goes too far. He's the first one to admit it.*

(From Apocalypse Now, *1979)*

AH—NOTHING SAYS "MALE" MORE THAN going to extremes. And it happens in fantasy football in so many ways. But first let me drift back for a moment to when times were not so extreme and fantasy football was only a fraction as popular and well known as it is today.

It's been quite a while since a co-worker dropped by my desk to invite me to join his "fantasy football league." Back in 1990, the world of fantasy football was much different from what it is today. I didn't even attend the draft because my father-in-law and I went to watch Cal beat Wisconsin 28–8 that day. I just made a ranking of players using the 1989 stats found in an Athlon NFL magazine and then had my friend pick the team. I somehow won second place that year and I was forever hooked. I also started what would become a long and glorious history of reaching the championship and then losing it thanks to inopportune injuries on my squad or career best games from my opponent's players (ah, but not *this* year).

Fantasy football at that time was almost entirely played by professional males who often worked in the Information Technology sector. Figure we were all good with statistics and computers anyway, throw in a sport that we loved, and it was a slam dunk. Back then fantasy football was more like a secret society that spoke a language that few outsiders understood. Our information sources were rather scarce as well. Outside of local coverage of the closest NFL team (which was very heavily raided in drafts), about all there was to go on were box scores after the games were played and the two or three football games that we could actually watch. *USA Today* devoted a small part of their sports section to the NFL on Thursdays and Fridays and we would all spend late-week lunches reading the one-sentence-per-team write-ups. They even had a thing called (whispering) *the NFL injury report*! Hey—it was all we had and we were giddy to have that much.

As a former programmer and systems engineer, I had an analytical and technical background that I applied to NFL football in those early years, and I spent hours upon hours analyzing, projecting, reviewing, and crunching numbers. Thanks to football, I became adept with spreadsheets, as have many others. I also loved to write, and like any good Texas boy, I always loved football over any other sport.

In 1996 at the annual EDS Fantasy Football League (EFFL) draft, my archrival, Whitney Walters, sat next to me while I covered my cheat sheet from his prying eyes. Having played in the league for six seasons, we had started a pattern of trading off championships each year. So it was with some surprise when he struck up a conversation with me discussing the scant information resources, which then ended with "you know, we should open a Web site."

The Internet was fairly new then. You either belonged to the AOL universe or you spent your time surfing from site to site using their links to go somewhere else. As someone who only slept about four hours a night and who had plenty of time to kill in the wee hours, I was certainly intrigued. At the time, there were really no fantasy football Web sites per se, just a couple of home pages where you could purchase weekly reports to be mailed or faxed to you. I began contributing to a free Web site named Fantasy Football

1996, which closed in the final month of the season as did many of the early fantasy football sites. I found myself spending all my free time writing detailed reviews of upcoming games with predictions of the outcome and projecting what I thought players would do. To my surprise, Whitney called me that January to resurrect the Web site idea.

I won't recount the early years of The Huddle since that was already well documented in Mark St. Amant's hilarious book, *Committed: Confessions of a Fantasy Football Junkie.* The Internet was like the Wild West and there were very few places to go for football information. We set up shop in 1997 with the intention of producing the sort of Web site that we wished existed and that would be a valuable resource for our fellow fantasy football fanatics. A place where we could offer our own advice and information while providing a forum for others to express themselves as well. Whitney and I put a lot of effort into the site considering that there were only around 100 visitors that first month. But since our little venture was only costing us $39.99 per month to host and we basically came free of charge, we kept working. And the next month we had 200 visitors. That became 400. Then 800 . . . 1,600 . . . 3,200 . . . By the end of the season, we were politely asked to leave our Internet provider because evidently $39.99 a month was never meant to involve server-crashing traffic.

Sure, we were literally paying money to work ourselves to death and still keep up at our day jobs. But it was truly a labor of love, the sort of work that you could not wait to do every day. Unlike most places, we offered our content free of charge if only because we had no idea how to charge for it—and above all, it was just a blast to do something that you loved and have it be so well received. Sort of that "not sure where this is heading, but man, we are really making great time" kind of situation.

No retrospective is complete without acknowledging our peers in the industry in the early days who became not only competitors but respected friends as well. William Del Pilar and Ryan Bonini

(KFFL), David Dodds (Mr. Football, now Footballguys), Mike Hall (MyFantasyLeague), Greg Kellogg (Kellogg's Komments), Bob Harris (TFL Report), Jim Lenz (Fantasy Insights), Sam and Adam Caplan (Fantasy Football Insider), Steve Cohen (footballin juries), Mike Nazarek (Fantasy Football Mastermind), John Hansen (FantasyGuru), Emil Kadlec (*Fantasy Football Pro Forecast* magazine), Ian Allen (*Fantasy Football Index* magazine), Dan Grogan (*Grogan's Magazine*), and Charlie Wiegert (CDM Fantasy Sports) were among the precious few resources in fantasy football during those early years. Each has his own story to tell and all were instrumental in taking what was once the happy hobby of a select few to now being a national phenomenon that borders on obsession for many people. They rate as the Henry Ford, Louis Chevrolet, David Buick, Horace Dodge, and Ransom Olds of the fantasy football industry.

While perhaps The Huddle could be bigger with a monopoly over fantasy advice and information (and yes, I daydream about it), even I must admit those early pioneers are a part of the reason fantasy football has become so popular and pervasive. In addition to being wise in the ways of football, they're all good guys when you get to know them too because they're smart, passionate, and just as devoted to a labor of love as we are at The Huddle. Rather different from what you get at the now ubiquitous "Big Corporate Sports" Web sites.

As we witnessed the ever-increasing number of fantasy football fans on the Internet, it did not take an MBA from Harvard to see that eventually there was going to be money to be made in the future. Like the mom-and-pop store owners in a small town, we knew it was only a matter of time before the big media players in sports would become our version of Wal-Mart and Target. In 1999, The Huddle was invited to supply Fox Sports with all of their fantasy football content prior to them taking it over and producing it themselves. By now, each of the "Big Boys"—ESPN, CBS SportsLine, Fox Sports, and Yahoo!—have rolled out their own fantasy offerings, usually with a league product, a contest or two, and some premium fantasy content. By virtue of their enormous existing audience and deep marketing pockets, they have already realized the sort of big profits that fills boardrooms with sloppy grins.

Fantasy football is no longer the unspoken bastard child of the NFL. It has become the black sheep turned into a rock star. It is the cash cow on the corporate farm. In the old days, it was *USA Today* and three games on Sunday. Now there is a flood of information and you can watch every single football game thanks to the NFL Sunday Ticket.

In Major League Baseball, the MLBPA signed over licensing rights to a third party called the MLBAM (Major League Baseball Advanced Media), which in turn is owned by MLB teams. In a well-publicized action, they began requiring licenses from companies that used public domain statistics to produce fantasy baseball contests and league software. Then they opted to allow only those biggest companies a chance to become licensed while denying such to all others. They later recanted to allow the smallest of sites to continue to operate without legal action because ostensibly they were still "for the little guy."

The National Football League Players Association is joining their baseball brethren with more than a little vested interest. The MLBAM court case found in favor of the defendant to keep names and statistics public, but there will likely be appeals and other attempts to control information. It's all about the Benjamins now. That and quarterly earnings reports and lawyers and courts. No one should blame them really. It is a pretty sweet deal when public domain statistics are freely doled out to any media source willing to print them and yet any contest or league management product is either required to pay exorbitant fees or is denied a license with a threat of a lawsuit if they continue. Ironically, those contests and league products have been instrumental in bringing football to an all-time high level of popularity. The broadcasting rights alone in the NFL recently went for $17.6 billion coughed up by ESPN, CBS, and Fox.

So now the largest percentage of fantasy footballers no longer play on league management Web sites that were started a decade ago and improved annually by fantasy football fanatics, with an eye for improving the experience and an ear for listening to their customers. They are instead cranked out by programmers paid by the hour—customer service calls may end up in Brazil where the term "football" spawns questions about the World Cup. But it works, for the most part, and most people don't know any better anyway.

As someone who has been passionately involved in fantasy football for the better part of two decades now, I am hardly concerned about being smaller than the Big Guys. We may all only get the relative trickle left over after the corporate buckets are removed from the tap but that's okay. I actually earn a living doing what I love to do and something that I actually paid for the privilege to do for many years. Like anyone else who loves fantasy football, I will always be concerned about the enjoyment and experience that people have when they play. All things being equal, I would much rather handcraft a Porsche than manage a Ford plant. I just have fears that a bad driving experience will turn away people from the product. And I shudder when I get an e-mail from someone wanting to know why my projections, which are the product of almost two decades of research, analysis, knowledge, and skills, do not match up with what a cartoon character says over at a corporate fantasy site. It's the way of the world, I suppose.

So where does fantasy football go from here? It has and will continue to be co-opted by well-moneyed interests with legal staffs. Like all industries, it will continue to lean more and more toward the big corporations with a concern toward the buck rather than the connection between people who play fantasy sports as a source of entertainment and competition. There is already so much information out there that the biggest challenge is not locating news but deciding what is actually fact and what is hype and what is merely the result of the 25th microphone shoved into a coach's face on the same day. In the old days, fantasy football resources were scarce.

Now—Google returns over 24 million results for the search term "fantasy football." I remember when it was less than a hundred. And there was no Google.

But for all the negatives, potential and realized, fantasy football has exploded in a way that exceeds all expectations. In the early days, I hated telling people about my unusual vocation. Here is an actual conversation that I once had:

Him: So, what do you do for a living?

Me: I co-own a Web site with a friend and help produce the content.

Him: Oh, so is it a porn Web site or a gambling Web site?

Me: Um . . . I run a fantasy football Web site.

Him: Oh, okay . . . So you're saying that it's both?

Our hobby was not helped by the genius who first called it "fantasy" football. Perform an Internet search on the word "fantasy" and everything is about dragons, elves, and hobbits. Take the adult filter off and it turns into a wide array of athletic yet completely non-football-related activities. I used to tell people that I was a plumber or a fireman just to keep the conversation going. Fortunately now, fantasy sports is popular enough that most people understand what it is, at least to the point that it is not about pornographic gambling.

So here we are, fantasy football growing by leaps and bounds while corporations, players associations, and courtrooms start making the decisions and calling the shots. The pursuit that so many of us started long ago has changed dramatically. Information comes so fast and is so voluminous that it's a question of sorting it out more than finding it. We've gone from being the Wild West where we waited for a week to get a letter from home to standing in the middle of Times Square during New Year's Eve. Companies have taken notice and shut down Internet access or even banned fantasy football from the workplace altogether.

Fantasy football has been taken to the extreme by corporations running it while other corporations go to the other extreme and prohibit it. Information is now on overload and groupthink and empty hype run rampant. On the other side of the monitor, what sort of fantasy football addict have you become? Has fantasy football gone to the extreme for you as well? While leagues are now populated with people of all ages, races, backgrounds, and both genders, it still is largely a middle-aged, professional male pursuit. That means we must constantly avoid perhaps the one thing that the Y chromosome seems to naturally promote—discovering a good thing and then taking it too far.

How many leagues are you in? It is a natural progression once you begin to gain knowledge and skills to add more leagues to your season. I've played in up to a dozen before. I know of people that at least claim to be in close to 20. But do you do as well as you once did in fewer leagues? More importantly, are you enjoying it is much as you once did? Does fantasy football add to the value of your life or does it detract from other areas? What does fantasy football mean to you now?

Think back to what it was that attracted you to the hobby. Was it the chance to juggle a dozen leagues and spend excessive time poring over so much information that eventually it begins to contradict itself? Does your family ever come second to fantasy football? Has anyone ever questioned how healthy your pursuit is to all concerned? Did you become involved in fantasy football for these reasons?

Probably not.

When I sat down to write this book, my intention was never to explain about the basics of fantasy football. I wrote this for the audience of devoted, passionate fantasy footballers out there who wanted to take their game to The Next Level. Many of you could well be in that category of being obsessed with fantasy football.

Some of you could possibly get that way. Hopefully most of you take it as a pleasurable way to involve yourself in professional football and won't allow it to ever be a problem.

Think back to what fantasy football was when you started. I am sure that each of you already enjoyed watching professional football. I imagine every one of us once played the same game as kids on a rock-strewn field where we pretended to be our heroes. Fantasy football was a way to once again interact with a game that brought us joy and entertainment. We got to test our skills in evaluating talent and putting together a team. We assembled a league of friends and co-workers and promoted interaction with each other in a way that was just plain fun. We competed with each other over the course of four months in order to win a couple of bucks and get the league trophy that was an empty beer can with a cloverleaf painted on it. We found Internet message boards where we could stay in contact with others like us, share information, and bring yet more enjoyment to our hobby.

In the end as it was in the beginning, fantasy football will never be about corporate profits, lawsuits, questions of gambling, wasting company time, or overloading yourself with so many leagues that it all becomes work instead of play. It's about people like you and me interacting in a fantasy league that should be entertaining, exciting, pleasurable, and maybe just a little frustrating. If it isn't fun—you need to cut back until it returns to being a positive aspect in your life and not an obsession that negatively impacts you and the people around you. It's easy to go overboard—heck, we're guys and that's pretty much what we do until we have the epiphany that we need to reel it back in a bit.

Realize that we are all ambassadors of the game to those who have never played. It is through our actions that people form their perceptions both at home and at work. I don't need to sell you on the hobby. But we need to recognize how we promote it to the rest of the world. We need to ensure that it is only a positive in our lives and through that a positive to other people, family first and foremost. Be a good spouse, parent, and friend long before you are a great fantasy team owner. Let it be something that brings us together and makes this hectic, demanding world just a little better than it was yesterday. After all my words, tools, tips, and techniques, it really all comes down to just one thing:

Rule 25

You are the future of fantasy football.

Have a great season . . . DMD

Glossary

3-10-20 Analysis   Reviewing the previous season's results for fantasy points of all starting positions and comparing the average points scored for the top three, fourth through 10th, and 11th through 20th highest scores among all positions.

Advanced Draft Tracker   A simple matrix used during a draft to record what positions have been filled by each team.

Consistency   How often a player scores close to his average during games that season.

The Dorey Rule   Draft as if the season only lasted the first six weeks. Select players based on the most favorable match-ups for those initial weeks of the season to gain an advantage over the rest of the league.

Ease of Schedule   The breakdown of how often fantasy positions for an NFL team will face defenses that rank in the top 10 for allowing fantasy points in that position or the top 10 defenses for minimizing fantasy points allowed. Unlike strength of schedule, which measures the won/loss record of opponents for an NFL team, the ease of schedule measures how many "good" and "bad" match-ups a player is facing in the upcoming season.

Flex Position   The use of an extra starting position each week, which can be drawn from more than one position (most often running back or wide receiver).

LAG (League Analysis and Graphing)   Analysis tool using a spreadsheet and line graphs to display and analyze the effects of league scoring on the various starting positions based upon the previous season's fantasy scores in that scoring scenario.

Mock Draft   A draft that is conducted with no intention of turning it into a real league; a practice draft to try out different strategies and review where individual players are being drafted.

Projection   The assignment of exact statistics for what a player could produce in a future season based upon what he has done in the past. Should describe the most likely outcome.

RBBC (Running-Back-by-Committee)   When an NFL team employs more than one running back in their rushing attack with enough frequency that no single player has more than 65 percent of all running back plays.

Reliability   How often a player scores close to his average over *several* seasons.

Replacement Running Back   A running back who assumes the full-time role whenever the primary running back cannot play. This player may have little or no playing time until called to be the replacement for an absent primary back.

Risk   The consideration of how likely a player is to produce significantly lower fantasy points than projected; the opposite of upside.

Sleeper   Any player who is drafted and then delivers far in excess of the suggested value from where he was selected. Usually a player who becomes a top fantasy player in his position after a year where he did not deliver enough fantasy points to warrant a fantasy start and is not popularly expected to perform so well.

Standard Fantasy Scoring   The most basic fantasy scoring scenario. Awards one point per each 10 yards rushed or received, and one point per 20 yards passed. All touchdowns count as six points with the exception of passing touchdowns, which are worth four points. Kickers receive their same NFL points and defenses gain one point per sack or turnover recovered and two points per safety recorded.

Stud Repeatability   Consideration of how often a top scoring player in his position repeats his performance the following season.

Tiers   The grouping of players within a position who share a similar expected fantasy value. This allows a faster review of the remaining available players in a fantasy draft so that better strategic decisions can be made in drafting from one position while delaying drafting from another.

Upside   The consideration of how likely a player is to produce significantly higher fantasy points than projected; the opposite of risk.

Appendix

TABLE I

QB'S WHO BECAME TOP 5 AFTER RANKING BELOW 20TH THE PREVIOUS YEAR

Year	Name	What Happened?
1997	Kordell Stewart	Two years on bench or as receiver, first season as a starter. Had only 17 passing TD's but added 11 rushing TD's. Defenses figured it out and he never came close to repeating again.
1997	Jeff George	First season in Oakland after a year wearing out his welcome in Atlanta.
1998	Randall Cunningham	Second season in Minnesota, first as a starter.
1998	Peyton Manning	Rookie year with Colts. The proverbial exception to the rule.
1999	Kurt Warner	First year with Rams as starter when Trent Green was injured that summer. This was legendary and pure "situation."
1999	Brad Johnson	First season in Washington after wearing out welcome in Minnesota.
2000	Daunte Culpepper	First year playing after a year of seasoning on the bench.
2000	Donovan McNabb	First full year as a starter after playing 12 games as a rookie.
2001	Aaron Brooks	First full year as a starter after playing eight games as a sophomore. Rookie year on bench in Green Bay.
2002	Michael Vick	First year as a starter after playing eight games as a rookie. Ran in eight touchdowns and gained 777 rushing yards.
2002	Drew Bledsoe	First year as a starter in Buffalo after wearing out welcome in New England.
2003	Marc Bulger	First year as a starter after playing in seven games as a sophomore. Rookie year on bench in St. Louis.
2005	Eli Manning	First full year as a starter after playing nine games as a rookie.
2006	Jon Kitna	First year as starter in Detroit in a Mike Martz offense.

APPENDIX

TABLE II

QUARTERBACK BREAKOUT SEASONS

Name	Drafted	Draft Slot	Break-out Season	Age	Original Team?	Full Seasons	Years Played	Years with Team	Total Yards	Total TD's
Peyton Manning	1998	1.01	1998	22	Y	1	1	1	3,801	26
Drew Bledsoe	1993	1.01	1994	22	Y	1	2	2	4,595	27
Daunte Culpepper	1999	1.11	2000	23	Y	1	2	2	4,377	40
Jeff Garcia*	1999	NA	2000	30	N	1	2	2	4,692	35
Eli Manning	2004	1.01	2005	24	Y	1	2	2	3,842	25
Donovan McNabb	1999	1.02	2000	24	Y	1	2	2	3,994	27
Michael Vick	2001	1.01	2002	24	Y	1	2	2	3,713	24
Kurt Warner*	1998	NA	1999	28	Y	1	2	2	4,445	42
Aaron Brooks	1999	4.36	2001	25	N	1	3	2	4,190	23
Marc Bulger	2001	6.02	2003	26	Y	1	3	3	3,920	26
Matt Hasselbeck	1999	6.34	2003	28	N	1	5	3	3,966	28
Tom Brady	2000	6.33	2002	25	Y	2	3	3	3,874	28
Carson Palmer	2003	1.01	2005	25	Y	2	3	3	3,877	33
Trent Green	1993	8.26	2002	32	N	2	10	2	3,915	27
Rich Gannon	1987	4.14	1999	34	N	4	10	1	4,138	26
Steve McNair	1995	1.03	2001	28	Y	5	7	7	3,764	26
Jake Plummer	1997	2.12	2004	30	N	7	8	2	4,291	28

*Both Jeff Garcia and Kurt Warner were undrafted and had played in the CFL and in the Arena League respectively.

The most common breakout for quarterbacks came in his second season with his original team, but only after he had been little or not used in his first season. This underscores the importance of allowing the rookie to season on the bench for a year before handing him the reins.

TABLE III

TOP 5 RUNNING BACKS WHO WERE WORSE THAN 20TH THE PREVIOUS YEAR

Year	Name	What Happened?
1997	Napoleon Kaufman	First (and only) year when head coach Joe Bugel gave Kaufman the starting job and Harvey Williams was phased out after sharing equally in 1996.
1998	Fred Taylor	Rookie season for Taylor, who scored 14 touchdowns that year because head coach Tom Coughlin didn't pull him at the goal line.
1999	Edgerrin James	Rookie season and start of a great career.
1999	Stephen Davis	First season as a starter after Terry Allen finally left.
2000	Mike Anderson	Rookie season as a starter when Terrell Davis was injured.
2000	Ahman Green	First year as a starter in Green Bay after two seasons in Seattle fumbling or warming the bench.
2001	Priest Holmes	First year as a starter in Kansas City after four years in Baltimore as a backup player.
2001	Shaun Alexander	First year as a starter when Ricky Watters was injured.
2002	Clinton Portis	Rookie season in Denver when Mike Anderson was moved to full-back.
2005	Larry Johnson	When Priest Holmes went down, Johnson never stopped running. First year "out of the doghouse."
2006	Frank Gore	First year as full-time starter in San Francisco when Kevan Barlow was traded away. Also first year of Norv Turner offense.

TABLE IV

6TH TO 10TH BEST RUNNING BACKS WHO WERE LESS THAN 20TH THE PREVIOUS YEAR

Year	Name	What Happened?
1997	Corey Dillon	Rookie season after Ki-Jana Carter was injured.
1998	Robert Edwards	Rookie season before injury on the sands of Hawaii.
1999	Dorsey Levens	After big year in 1997, missed much of 1998 injured. Came back for a career-best year.
1999	Charlie Garner	First season as a full-time starter in San Francisco after being a part-timer in Philadelphia for the five previous years.
2000	Fred Taylor	After missing much of 1999 with a knee injury, came back for a career-best-yardage year.
2001	LaDainian Tomlinson	Rookie season in San Diego.
2002	Travis Henry	Second year for the Bills, when he went from 213 carries (2001) to 325 carries (2002).
2002	Deuce McAllister	First year as a starter in New Orleans after watching Ricky Williams for one year.
2004	Corey Dillon	First year with the Patriots after falling out of favor with the Bengals.
2004	Rudi Johnson	First season given the reins after Dillon left. Had success the previous season but shared with Dillon.
2004	Willis McGahee	"Rookie" year with the Bills after recuperating in 2003 from a knee injury.
2005	LaMont Jordan	First year as a starter after four years as backup to Curtis Martin in New York.
2005	Mike Anderson	With Clinton Portis gone, reassumed starting role for the first time in three years.
2006	Maurice Jones-Drew	Rookie season with the Jaguars with all the goal line duty.

There were 25 players over a 10-year period that went from a sub-20th-level performance to a top 10 or even a top five season. The one commonality? Literally all were in new situations. The first key to finding a sleeper back is either to find a guy with enough opportunity to have a shot at a big year or at least to be a backup player on a team that has a great offensive line and scheme so that if his number is called, he can plug in and continue to keep the running game on pace.

TABLE V

RUNNING BACK BREAKOUT SEASONS

Name	Drafted	Draft Slot	Break-out Season	Age	Original Team?	Full Seasons	Years Played	Years with Team	Total Yards	Total TD's
Curtis Martin	1995	3.10	1995	22	Y	1	1	1	1,748	15
Corey Dillon	1997	2.13	1997	23	Y	1	1	1	1,388	10
Edgerrin James	1999	1.04	1999	21	Y	1	1	1	2,139	17
Shaun Alexander	2000	1.19	2001	24	Y	1	2	2	1,661	16
Mike Anderson	2000	NA	2000	27	Y	1	1	1	1,656	15
LaDainian Tomlinson	2001	1.05	2001	22	Y	1	1	1	1,603	10
Clinton Portis	2002	2.19	2002	21	Y	1	1	1	1,872	17
Larry Johnson	2003	1.27	2005	26	Y	1	3	3	2,093	21
Willis McGahee	2003	1.23	2004	23	Y	1	1	2	1,297	13
Rudi Johnson	2001	5.04	2004	25	Y	2	4	4	1,538	12
Domanick Davis	2003	4.04	2004	24	Y	2	2	2	1,776	14
Tiki Barber	1997	2.06	2000	25	Y	3	4	4	1,725	9
Thomas Jones	2000	1.07	2005	27	N	5	6	2	1,478	9
LaMont Jordan	2001	2.18	2005	27	N	5	5	1	1,588	11

Running backs will tend to break out immediately when they are given a starting role, whether that comes in their rookie season or as late as their fifth or sixth year, as with LaMont Jordan and Thomas Jones respectively. Most running backs had their big year with their original team and only in the case of Jordan and Jones did they break out with another team. Priest Holmes is another example of an older player exploding on the season, but even he was in his first season with a new team.

TABLE VI

ROOKIE YEAR STATS AND RANKS FOR FIRST-ROUND RUNNING BACKS

Player	Total Yards	Total TD's	RB Rank*	Games Played
LaDainian Tomlinson ('01-SD)	1,593	10	7	16
Joseph Addai ('06-IND)	1,406	8	11	16
Jamal Lewis ('00-BAL)	1,660	6	16	16
Reggie Bush ('06-NO)	1,306	8	16	16
Carnell Williams ('05-TB)	1,259	6	19	14
Kevin Jones ('04-DET)	1,313	6	21	15
Ronnie Brown ('05-MIA)	1,139	5	23	15
William Green ('02-CLE)	1,000	6	27	16
Laurence Maroney ('06-NE)	939	7	28	14
Ron Dayne ('00-NYG)	781	5	29	16
Michael Bennett ('01-MIN)	908	3	30	13
Steven Jackson ('04-STL)	864	4	33	14
DeAngelo Williams ('06-CAR)	814	2	41	13
Thomas Jones ('00-ARZ)	581	2	42	14
T. J. Duckett ('02-ATL)	568	4	42	12
Shaun Alexander ('00-SEA)	352	2	55	16
Deuce McAllister ('01-NO)	257	2	67	11
Cedric Benson ('05-CHI)	275	0	86	9
Larry Johnson ('03-KC)	87	1	104	6
Trung Canidate ('00-STL)	10	0	—	2
Willis McGahee ('03-BUF)**	0	0	—	0
Chris Perry ('04-CIN)	34	0	—	2

*Ranking considers standard scoring of 0.1 point per yard gained and six-point TD's against all RB's that year.
**Willis McGahee actually sat out his first season recovering from a knee injury but returned in 2004 to gain 1,297 yards and 13 TDs.

While rookie running backs are always coveted, their actual production their first year has not been all that impressive since 2000. No arguing that Tomlinson had a big rookie season and several others did end up with freshman years that would deservedly make them be your second starting running back. But considering the optimism spawned with rookie runners, more often than not they are not ending up delivering on expectations.

Two thousand six was the best year for rookie running backs in many years when both Joseph Addai and Reggie Bush turned in performances worthy of being a fantasy starter; but both players came on strong in the second half of the season and had one monster game to pump up their overall statistics. With Maurice Jones-Drew turning in a top 10 year as a second-rounder, history says that 2006 was a major aberration and not something to count on in future seasons.

TABLE VII

TOP 5 WIDE RECEIVERS WHO WERE WORSE THAN 20TH THE PREVIOUS YEAR

Year	Name	What Happened?
2000	Rod Smith	Career-high yardage in the middle of his six straight years with over 1,000 yards. Had decent year in '99 and a final big year in '01.
2000	Terrell Owens	Had good year in '98, hurt in '99; then Jerry Rice finally hit the wall in '00, letting Owens take over. Last season of Rice, changing of the guard, and Owens had four more monster years after this.
2000	Derrick Alexander	Third year in Kansas City—truly a magic year not repeated. Second year with Elvis Grbac during his only good season—Gonzo also exploded that year. Good season with two monster games.
2002	Eric Moulds	First year with Drew Bledsoe. Had been big in '98 in first year with Doug Flutie. Both QB's relied heavily on him in those two years; otherwise he was just an average possession receiver.
2002	Hines Ward	First year with Tommy Maddox as QB, and running game was unusually bad that year. Mainly Ward became the TD guy while both he and Plaxico Burress had big yardage. In '05, had an average 1,000-yard season but became the touchdown target once again.
2003	Anquan Boldin	Rookie for pass-happy team despite not even being the first WR drafted by the Cardinals. Legendary and extremely rare breakout in rookie season.
2004	Muhsin Muhammad	While Boldin holds the youth record for surprises, Muhammad takes the veteran one. Second year of Jake Delhomme, no real running game thanks to injuries and Steve Smith injured as well.
2005	Steve Smith	His second season with Delhomme. Rushing still not average but more than anything he took everything that Muhammad left behind when he departed. Surprise in that he came off a broken leg in '04. Was the only real WR option.
2005	Larry Fitzgerald	Went from very nice rookie season to great second year. Pass-happy offense with league-worst running game.
2005	Santana Moss	Had breakout year in '03 with the Jets and then at Washington had the same big year with long passes in '05. Was the only real WR option in Washington as he was in '03 in New York after Lavernues Coles left.
2005	Joey Galloway	Career-best season 11 years after being drafted. Stayed healthy and was the only real WR option with Michael Clayton turning back into a hurt pumpkin. First 1,000+ season in six years.

TABLE VIII

6TH TO 10TH BEST WIDE RECEIVERS WHO WERE LESS THAN 20TH THE PREVIOUS YEAR

Year	Name	What Happened?
2000	Torry Holt	Broke out in his second year in a pass-happy offense. Learning curve was shortened by his talent and the volume of passes that St. Louis threw.
2000	Joe Horn	Four years in Kansas City, only had 53 catches and almost never played in his first two seasons. Blew up in first year with the Saints. Soft schedule and big ending to year to nudge him up.
2001, 2003	Derrick Mason	Solid possession receiver who tacked on extra touchdowns for two years to nudge up. Never worse than 1,000 yards and five TD's as a Titan from '01 to '04.
2002	Amani Toomer	Solid possession receiver who had a freak 204-yard, three-TD game to end '02 and nudge up for career-best season.
2002	Peerless Price	Around 700 yards and three TD's every year except '02 and first year of Bledsoe gave him monster stats by midseason before he once again returned to be only an average #2 WR in Buffalo.
2002	Plaxico Burress	Third-year breakout season after a solid second year. Bad-rushing, high-passing game in '02 under Tommy Maddox and partially under Kordell Stewart. Had a monster 253-yard, two-TD game against Atlanta that truly made his season.
2002, 2004	Donald Driver	This is the receiver who Brett Favre created. Two nine-touchdown years when Favre was on, and even Javon Walker in '04 did not diminish his year. Down year in 2003 and still only five TD's in 2005 despite being the only WR of note that year.
2003	Darrell Jackson	Nine touchdowns pushed him up in '03, but Jackson has been an excellent possession WR since 2001 when healthy.
2003, 2005	Chris Chambers	Solid possession WR that had 11-TD years in '03 and '05 while normally only has about 900 yards and seven TD's. Biggest years are when there is no productive #2 and even in bad '04 still easily led Miami in receiving.
2004	Drew Bennett	Had his career-best magic year with a three-game stretch of eight TD's and 517 yards. Otherwise just another sub-average year.
2004	Reggie Wayne	Breakout season in '04 when Peyton Manning constantly threw but back to 1,000 yards and five scores when they started running again in '05. With great quarterback who was on a torrid pace.
2003, 2005	Anquan Boldin	Pass-happy offense had Boldin skyrocket as a rookie when there were no other WR's on the team, and in '05 returned from injury in '04 to post more big numbers. Lack of any running game meshed well with tons of passes to Boldin and Larry Fitzgerald—almost exclusively.
2006	Javon Walker	Missed '05 season injured and then traded to Denver to be primary wideout.

TABLE IX

WIDE RECEIVER BREAKOUT SEASONS

Name	Drafted	Draft Slot	Break-out Season	Age	Original Team?	Full Seasons	Years Played	Years with Team	Total Yards	Total TD's
Anquan Boldin	2003	2.23	2003	23	Y	1	1	1	1,377	8
Larry Fitzgerald	2004	1.03	2005	22	Y	2	2	2	1,409	10
Torry Holt	1999	1.06	2000	25	Y	2	2	2	1,635	6
Santana Moss	2001	1.16	2003	24	Y	2	3	3	1,105	10
Joe Horn	1996	5.03	2000	28	N	2	5	1	1,340	8
Chris Chambers	2001	2.21	2003	25	Y	3	3	3	963	11
Joey Galloway	1995	1.08	1997	27	Y	3	3	3	1,049	12
Chad Johnson	2001	2.05	2003	26	Y	3	3	3	1,355	10
Terrell Owens	1996	3.28	1998	25	Y	3	3	3	1,097	14
Javon Walker	2002	1.20	2004	27	Y	3	3	3	1,382	12
Donald Driver	1999	7.07	2002	28	Y	4	3	4	1,064	9
Drew Bennett	2001	Und	2004	26	Y	4	4	4	1,247	11
Marvin Harrison	1996	1.19	1999	27	Y	4	4	4	1,663	12
Reggie Wayne	2001	1.30	2004	26	Y	4	4	4	1,210	12
Steve Smith	2001	3.12	2005	25	Y	4	5	5	1,563	12
Hines Ward	1998	3.30	2002	26	Y	4	5	5	1,329	12
Muhsin Muhammad	1996	2.13	2004	31	Y	9	9	9	1,405	16

While everyone is aware that third-year wide receivers are the stereotypical breakout players, the reality is that fourth-year players are actually more likely to experience that big jump in production, and several have made that leap as early as their second season. It's more about talent and situation than mere opportunity.

TABLE X

ROOKIE YEAR STATS AND RANKS FOR FIRST-ROUND WIDEOUTS

First-Round Wide Receivers	Total Yards	Total TD's	WR Rank*	Games Played
Michael Clayton ('04-TB)	1,193	7	13	16
Andre Johnson ('03-HOU)	976	4	23	16
Lee Evans ('04-BUF)	843	9	24	16
Donte Stallworth ('02-NO)	564	8	29	13
Roy Williams ('04-DET)	817	8	29	14
Larry Fitzgerald ('04-ARZ)	780	8	30	16
Rod Gardner ('01-WAS)	741	4	39	16
Matt Jones ('05-JAX)	432	5	50	16
Braylon Edwards ('05-CLE)	512	3	59	10
Mark Clayton ('05-BAL)	471	2	61	14
David Terrell ('01-CHI)	415	4	62	16
Roddy White ('05-ATL)	446	3	64	16
Koren Robinson ('01-SEA)	536	1	65	16
Bryant Johnson ('03-ARZ)	438	1	68	15
Troy Williamson ('05-MIN)	372	2	79	14
Ashley Lelie ('02-DEN)	525	2	80	16
Freddie Mitchell ('01-PHI)	283	1	81	15
Reggie Wayne ('01-IND)	345	0	86	13
Charles Rogers ('03-DET)	243	3	89	5
Mike Williams ('05-DET)	350	1	91	14
Javon Walker ('02-GB)	319	1	95	15
Reggie Williams ('04-JAX)	268	1	97	16
Rashaun Woods ('04-SF)	160	1	111	13
Michael Jenkins ('04-ATL)	119	0	136	16
Santana Moss ('01-NYJ)	40	0	na	5

*Ranking considers standard scoring of 0.1 point per yard gained and six-point TD's against all WR's that year.

This review did not quite go back far enough to catch Randy Moss, which is a good thing—he was a freak in all ways because a top rookie wideout is an extreme rarity. Since 2000, only Michael Clayton had a truly notable rookie year and only three wideouts had any true value as a starter for a fantasy team. Wide receivers are being pushed into duty earlier every season but that doesn't mean that rookies are showing up with much fantasy relevance. Anquan Boldin was a second-round selection by the Cardinals in 2003 and was drafted after Bryant Johnson (ranked 68th that year).

TABLE XI

TIGHT END BREAKOUT SEASONS

Name	Drafted	Draft Slot	Break- out Year	Original Team?	Full Seasons	Years Played	Years with Team	Total Yards	Total TD's
Jeremy Shockey	2002	1.14	2002	Y	1	1	1	894	2
Desmond Clark	1999	6.10	2001	Y	2	3	3	566	6
Chris Cooley	2004	3.18	2005	Y	2	2	2	774	7
Alge Crumpler	2001	2.04	2002	Y	2	2	2	455	5
Bubba Franks	2000	1.14	2001	Y	2	2	2	322	9
Antonio Gates	2003	NA	2004	Y	2	2	2	964	13
Todd Heap	2001	1.31	2002	Y	2	2	2	836	6
Jason Witten	2003	3.04	2004	Y	2	2	2	980	6
Frank Wycheck	1993	6.20	1996	N	2	4	2	511	6
Tony Gonzalez	1997	1.13	1999	Y	3	3	3	849	11
Randy McMichael	2002	4.16	2004	Y	3	3	3	791	4
Shannon Sharpe	1990	7.27	1993	Y	3	4	4	995	9
Jermaine Wiggins	2000	NA	2004	N	3	5	1	705	4
Marcus Pollard	1995	NA	2001	Y	4	6	6	739	8

The most common year for a breakout tight end is obviously when he is playing in his second full season as a starter. The tight ends who required three or four years to break out mostly were in years prior to the breakout season for tight ends of 2004 and 2005—the good players are not given as many seasons to step up as they once did. Breakout tight ends were drafted from several deep rounds, but those mostly happened prior to 2000.

TABLE XII

ROOKIE YEAR STATS AND RANKS FOR FIRST-ROUND TIGHT ENDS

Player	Total Yards	Total TD's	TE Rank*	Games Played
Jeremy Shockey ('02-NYG)	864	2	3	15
Heath Miller ('05-PIT)	459	6	11	16
Bubba Franks ('00-GB)	363	1	20	16
Vernon Davis ('06-SF)	265	3	22	9
Jerramy Stevens ('02-SEA)	252	3	23	12
Dallas Clark ('03-IND)	340	1	24	10
Todd Heap ('01-BAL)	206	1	31	12
Anthony Becht ('00-NYJ)	114	2	34	14
Daniel Graham ('02-NE)	150	1	42	11
Marcedes Lewis ('06-JAX)	126	1	46	9
Kellen Winslow ('04-CLE)	50	0	78	2
Ben Watson ('04-NE)	16	0	89	2

*Ranking considers standard scoring of 0.1 point per yard gained and six-point TD's considering all TE's that year.

Here we see that tight ends selected in the first round have a very spotty record in delivering fantasy value during their rookie season. Only Jeremy Shockey had a season that made him worthy of being a fantasy starter and that happened in 2002 before the increase in tight ends' scoring. After the top 10 tight ends, there is almost no advantage between having the 11th or 20th best in fantasy terms. Rookie tight ends are so rarely good in their first season that avoiding them is by far the safest bet.

TABLE XIII

NFL RANKINGS (1–32) FOR TOTAL PLACEKICKING POINTS—5-YEAR SAMPLE

TM	Avg	2001	2002	2003	2004	2005	TM	Avg	2001	2002	2003	2004	2005
DEN	6	3	9	6	2	9	SD	16	26	5	26	10	12
IND	7	2	19	2	7	5	TEN	18	23	14	3	26	23
PIT	8	4	8	19	3	7	BUF	18	29	12	31	9	10
PHI	10	9	2	9	5	24	CAR	19	25	30	5	28	5
BAL	10	8	22	4	8	10	MIN	19	31	15	16	19	16
STL	12	1	24	1	25	7	MIA	20	20	13	21	32	14
GB	12	4	15	4	6	29	ARI	20	21	29	32	16	2
NE	12	17	11	10	1	20	CLE	20	22	20	23	17	20
SEA	12	17	11	8	12	13	NYJ	21	19	16	27	14	29
KC	13	27	14	7	11	4	WAS	21	18	27	18	24	18
NYG	14	16	17	15	20	1	CHI	22	13	23	14	31	28
ATL	14	7	1	26	21	17	SF	22	15	24	18	29	25
NO	15	18	12	3	15	25	JAX	23	28	25	25	22	15
OAK	15	6	5	22	13	29	DAL	24	26	32	20	23	20
CIN	15	30	28	12	4	3	DET	24	27	21	24	18	32
TB	16	5	10	6	30	27	HOU	26	—	31	28	27	18

This table shows a sample of five years of total placekicking points scored by teams, and is a useful tool in evaluating kickers for the next season when it is kept up each year. While kickers will obviously vary from season to season, at least those around the top 10 tended to stay in the top 10 and those in the bottom 15 were pretty safe bets to remain unworthy of a fantasy start.

TABLE XIV

NATURAL RUNNING BACK TIERS FROM ACTUAL FANTASY POINTS

	1996	1997	1998	1999	2000	2001	2002	2003	2004	2005
1	281	320	361	316	372	337	365	365	297	360
2	275	294	313	315	332	269	317	337	293	333
3	264	253	283	254	284	256	299	336	282	302
4	250	232	266	254	252	255	281	303	271	301
5	237	218	265	230	246	236	267	271	255	266
6	236	211	241	221	240	225	262	262	252	235
7	221	201	219	212	240	212	258	257	248	224
8	203	199	217	203	232	211	251	228	219	223
9	191	197	215	202	231	208	249	222	201	200
10	189	188	202	193	231	185	222	214	199	199
11	177	188	196	185	224	180	214	210	195	195
12	173	186	196	182	223	180	212	203	194	183
13	173	185	186	179	218	172	211	179	192	171
14	167	176	182	174	210	164	205	179	189	170

This table shows that natural tiers do occur. Using standard scoring for fantasy running backs over a 10-year period, the top 14 scores are shown and shaded according to where natural tiers break.

TABLE XV

DIFFERENCE BETWEEN USING 16 WEEKS VS. STRATEGICALLY CULLING OUT WEEKS

Team	Pre-Cull	Post-Cull	Pre-Rank	Post-Rank	Diff	Team	Pre-Cull	Post-Cull	Pre-Rank	Post-Rank	Diff
SEA	13.6	14.0	1	1	0	ARI	18.9	17.6	20	17	3
CAR	14.3	12.6	2	2	0	CLE	20.1	17.9	24	18	6
CHI	14.3	14.1	3	3	0	NO	19.2	18.3	22	19	3
JAX	15.0	14.7	5	4	1	NYG	18.2	19.0	17	20	-3
DEN	14.8	14.8	4	5	-1	PHI	19.0	19.1	21	21	0
SD	15.9	15.6	8	6	2	WAS	18.8	19.5	19	22	-3
PIT	15.5	15.7	6	7	-1	TEN	19.5	19.9	23	23	0
KC	16.6	15.9	12	8	4	GB	18.3	20.0	18	24	-6
NE	16.8	16.1	13	9	4	OAK	22.1	20.1	28	25	3
BAL	17.2	16.1	14	10	4	DET	20.6	20.6	25	26	-1
IND	16.1	16.4	9	11	-2	SF	22.5	20.9	29	27	2
DAL	16.1	16.5	10	12	-2	NYJ	22.0	21.7	27	28	-1
CIN	15.7	16.6	7	13	-6	HOU	22.8	21.8	31	29	2
TB	16.3	16.9	11	14	-3	ATL	21.3	22.0	26	30	-4
MIA	17.2	17.1	15	15	0	BUF	22.5	22.0	30	31	-1
MIN	17.7	17.3	16	16	0	STL	23.6	25.0	32	32	0

Table shows where defenses ranked considering the full 16-game slate for defenses the previous season (Pre-Cull) and where they would rank after removing weeks one, two, 17, and the highest and lowest games allowed by that defense using a sample year. The changes are not too dramatic at the very top and become more pronounced starting with the eighth and later defenses.

The Next Level Rules

RULE 1

Draft your team for this year, not from last year.

RULE 2

Success is about team first,
positions second, and players third.

RULE 3

Statistics—whether actual or projected—
are only useful as guidelines.

RULE 4

Reception points mean fair drafts,
better teams, and more competition.

RULE 5

Teams change every year, even when they don't.

RULE 6

There is nothing as important
as having a genuine feel for the game.

RULE 7

QB Value = Talent × (Situation × 2) × Opportunity

RULE 8

RB Value = Talent × Situation × (Opportunity × 2)

RULE 9

The better your running back,
the more important that you own his backup.

RULE 10

WR Value = (Talent × 2) × Situation × Opportunity

RULE 11

TE Value = (Talent × 2) × (Situation × 2) × Opportunity

RULE 12

PK Value = Opportunity

RULE 13

DEF Value = 80% Talent + 20% Match-ups

RULE 14

Projections, by their very nature,
only describe one potential outcome.

RULE 15

Overreaching for an "upside" player
is the most common mistake.

RULE 16

True player value considers
reliability, risk, upside, and consistency.

THE NEXT LEVEL RULES

RULE 17

Never view any rankings until
you are finished with your own.

RULE 18

Always pay attention to the short side of your draft slot.

RULE 19

It's a fantasy draft, not a cafeteria.

RULE 20

The Dorey Rule:
Draft as if the season only lasted the first six weeks.

RULE 21

The top players in each position
are bigger than their schedule.

RULE 22

The schedule is bigger than the average player.

RULE 23

Never, ever be satisfied with your roster.
Churn for improvement.

RULE 24

Defensive match-ups are critical in the playoffs.

RULE 25

You are the future of fantasy football.

Index

management *(continued)*
  team, 250
  web site, 255
manual scoring, 207
match-ups
  defense, 237–238
  random, 160
methodology, 200–201
mid-draft, 79, 89–90, 193
missing games, 151, 239
mock drafts, xvi, 264
  cons of, 172–177
  fantasy team owner reliance on,
    175–176
  holding, 171
  LAG analysis comparing, 180
  outdated, 173–175
  pros of, 177–182
  review, 130–131, 182, 203
  value of positions shown by,
    178–179
multitasking, 246–247

natural tier, 16, 19, 28, 164–165,
  281
newbie, 197
NFL
  change within, xvii
  fantasy football v., 31–32, 257
  fantasy point production from, 13
  flux state of, 53

injury reality in, 99
  scouts, 96
  tight ends growing importance
    in, 124
  trends, xii
  two-back system used in, 43
  yards per carry standard in, 60
nondivisional rivals, 66

obsession, 245
offense
  complicated role on, 109
  components of, 57
  high-powered, 104
  kicker opportunity from offense,
    135
  running backs boost on, 3
  running backs way opened
    by, 83
  west coast, 127
offensive coordinator, 70
official listing, 185
off-season, xv–xvi, 1–48
online
  draft results, 176
  generating raw numbers, 7
opportunity, 91–92, 105, 271
  drafting, 231–232
  measuring, 137
  producing kicker, 138
owner. *See* fantasy team owners